Your Towns and Cities in t

Thurrock
in the Great War

Ken Porter and Stephen Wynn

Pen & Sword
MILITARY

First published in Great Britain in 2015 by
PEN & SWORD MILITARY
an imprint of
Pen and Sword Books Ltd
47 Church Street
Barnsley
South Yorkshire S70 2AS

ISBN 978 1 47382 310 5

Printed and bound in England
by CPI Group (UK) Ltd, Croydon, CR0 4YY

Typeset in Times New Roman by Chic Graphics

Pen & Sword Books Ltd incorporates the imprints of
Pen & Sword Archaeology, Atlas, Aviation, Battleground, Discovery,
Family History, History, Maritime, Military, Naval, Politics, Railways,
Select, Social History, Transport, True Crime, Claymore Press,
Frontline Books, Leo Cooper, Praetorian Press, Remember When,
Seaforth Publishing and Wharncliffe.

For a complete list of Pen and Sword titles please contact
Pen and Sword Books Limited
47 Church Street, Barnsley, South Yorkshire, S70 2AS, England
E-mail: enquiries@pen-and-sword.co.uk
Website: www.pen-and-sword.co.uk

Contents

The Authors

Stephen Wynn retired having served with Essex Police as a constable for thirty years. He is married to Tanya and has two sons and a daughter.

His interest in history has been fuelled by the fact that both his grandfathers served in and survived the First World War, one with the Royal Irish Rifles, the other in the Mercantile Navy, and his father was a member of the Royal Army Ordnance Corps during the Second World War. Both Stephen's sons, Luke and Ross, were members of the armed forces, serving five tours of Afghanistan between 2008 and 2013. Both were injured. This led to his first book, *Two Sons in a Warzone – Afghanistan: The True Story of a Father's Conflict* published in October 2010. He has also written three crime thrillers.

Ken and Stephen have collaborated on a previous book published in August 2012, *German POW Camp 266 – Langdon Hills*.

Ken is also retired, having spent his working life in accountancy as a finance director. These days he is a well-respected local historian of many years standing. Ken was born in Laindon in 1944; his passion has always been sport and history. At school he took an active part in athletics and football then in his early teens cricket took over and became his life's passion. Since retiring, history has taken precedence and his local knowledge is extensive. He became a leading enthusiast for the Basildon Heritage Group and Laindon and District Community Archive and gives talks to local societies. His interest in the First World War stems from his maternal grandfather, James Frederick Pitts, who saw active service.

Ken has been married to Carol for forty-eight years. They have three children and five grandchildren.

CHAPTER 1

The Great War

The first shots of the First World War were fired just after 0630 hours on the morning of 22 August 1914 by soldiers from C Squadron, 4th Dragoon Guards. One hundred and twenty men, commanded by Major Tom Bridges, were engaged in the opening exchange of the war at the village of Casteau in Belgium. Ironically, the last action of the war took place at the same village, just 50 yards away from where the opening shots were fired, on the morning of 11 November 1918, when members of the 11th Canadian Infantry were involved in fighting with German troops.

A stone memorial commemorates the initial action of the war and a plaque commemorates the last shots, making the village of Casteau an historic and well visited location for those interested in the First World War.

The Great War unleashed by those first shots would be a war like no other before it. It was war in its rawest sense; men would die in their thousands nearly every day. It would be bloody and brutal with many left broken both physically and mentally, a traumatic experience from which some would never recover. It wasn't only the soldiers who were affected; the close-knit communities from which they came suffered as well. In some cases families lost all their men folk; for some it meant the end of their family line.

However, in the early days of the war, there was a misplaced euphoria in Britain. 'It will be over by Christmas', was the belief of the masses. How wrong they would be.

By the time the war was over hardly a single community throughout

Britain remained untouched by it. Everybody was affected, from the young men who went off so cheerfully at first to fight for king and country, leaving parents, friends and families to worry, to those at home whose lives changed as a result of war production demands and food shortages.

The Defence of the Realm Act (DORA) placed more and more restrictions on people's lives than had ever been known before. As the war continued older men as well as married men with children, who had previously been exempt from having to enlist, were also being called up as the war continued far beyond the time it had been expected to continue.

Civilians were now literally dying in their beds in some parts of the country because of air raids carried out by German Zeppelins. The first such attack took place on the evening of 19 January 1915 when two German Zeppelin airships crossed the Norfolk coastline where they dropped their bombs over Great Yarmouth and Kings Lynn. That first raid claimed the lives of nine people.

There were a total of fifty-two Zeppelin raids on Britain during the war, mainly in 1915 and 1916, in which over 500 people were killed.

Besides suffering from German airship attacks, civilians were also feeling the effects of the increased naval losses at sea. Britain needed to import food from abroad to help feed its population, because without these much needed supplies getting through there would undoubtedly be hunger and starvation. As the war gathered momentum, so the losses at sea increased, which in return resulted in food shortages and the eventual need by the British Government to bring in rationing.

Nearly every community suffered during the First World War, including the people of Thurrock. The population of the area at the time was around 40,000 people which equates to about 8,000 families, many of whom were related to each other. With some 1,000 local men killed and hundreds more badly wounded, there weren't many families unaffected.

The First World War was the Great War, the war to end all wars – or so it was said – but as history would later reveal, that was destined not to be the case.

During the war the British Empire mobilized a total of 8,410,000 men; 908,371 either died or were killed; 2,090,212 men were wounded; 191,652 men were either missing or taken prisoner. In total 8,528,831 men from all sides were killed and another 37,466,904 men were wounded.[1]

These figures included 180,597 British and Empire troops who were wounded as a result of being gassed and a further 8,109 who were killed. How many of those wounded as a result of being gassed and who later died from their wounds after the war, is not recorded.

At sea the British lost 174 ships during the First World War, including battleships, cruisers, gunboats, torpedo boats, destroyers and submarines.

It also changed the structure of British society forever, decimating many aristocratic families and giving the masses a flavour of a better tomorrow, a taste which once acquired, wasn't readily going to be handed back to those who had previously owned it. The old ways had now gone forever. Many were no longer prepared to be subservient to those who had previously been their social masters or settle for second best, a way of life which they had previously accepted was to be their lot in life.

Of those who had been killed, wounded and injured during the war, the majority were from the working classes or the 'other ranks' as they were referred to. In the first months many officers came from society's élite, powerful and rich families but as the war went on that changed and there were many who rose from the ranks to become officers.

For most of those who enlisted during the war, it would have been the first time they had set foot on foreign soil. Some joined out of a desire to serve their country, others from a feeling of duty and honour. Some saw it as an adventure not to be missed, a way to break out from the restrictive drudgery and boredom of everyday life, as well as an opportunity to be part of something that would go down in history and that people would talk about for years to come. Each and every one of them was to be proved right.

England, Ireland, Scotland and Wales were once proud nations of tightly knit communities where the people looked out for one another. It is good to see that on 11 November each year that same spirit still exists, if only for a short period of time, whilst people pay their respects at war memorials all across the land. With the centenary of the Great War, this is a time for remembering those brave souls who gave their lives in the belief that it would ensure each one of us could continue to have a free and better tomorrow.

---

1 www.pbs.org/greatwar/resources/casdeath_pop.html

CHAPTER 2

Thurrock – A Brief History

In 1914 the district of Thurrock included the towns and villages of Fobbing, Stifford, Bulphan, Aveley, Purfleet, North Ockendon, South Ockendon, Corringham, Tilbury, East Tilbury, West Tilbury, Stanford-le-Hope, Horndon-on-the-Hill, Orsett, Langdon Hills, Mucking, Chadwell – St Mary, Little Thurrock, West Thurrock and Grays.

The area is situated in the south-west of Essex and sits between the north bank of the River Thames and the outskirts of London.

The name Thurrock dates from Saxon times but its meaning has two interpretations, neither of which could be described as being exactly complimentary. It either refers to the underneath of a boat where the bilge water collects, or a dung heap in a field. The name Grays, seems so much nicer.

The two names – Grays and Thurrock – have had a connection going back as far as 1195 when the Grays family purchased the manor of Thurrock from a local businessman.

The area has had a long-standing military connection and in more recent years, Coalhouse Fort at East Tilbury and Tilbury Fort further around the coast both played their part in the First and Second World Wars.

As a result of the British defeat of the French at the battle of Waterloo on 18 June 1815, the British Government became worried that the French would be looking for revenge. This resulted in a programme of work designed to strengthen Britain's docks and harbours around the country. The fortifications which were already in place at East Tilbury were improved and became known as the East

Tilbury Battery. The work was completed in 1855 providing the battery with some formidable fire power in the shape of seventeen 32-pounder smooth bore guns.

Because of further concerns that these defences were not up to scratch, the East Tilbury Battery was dismantled and work began on an even bigger and more imposing structure in the shape of Coalhouse Fort which remains in place to this day. One of the men in charge of supervising the building of the fort for a period of time was Lieutenant Colonel Gordon, of Khartoum fame.

However, because of improvements in artillery capabilities, by the time the fort was completed in 1874 it was almost obsolete. During the First World War, Coalhouse Fort's main use militarily was as an observation platform which kept a close watch on shipping travelling up the River Thames. During the intervening years it had been modernised with more powerful and effective guns along with a searchlight capability. It was also used by British troops as a forward holding area before they were sent to fight in France and Belgium.

Tilbury Docks were constructed as a result of an Act of Parliament in the early 1880s and were fully operational by 1886, opening the way for the trading of goods and the operating of passenger services to the rest of the world. It became part of the Port of London Authority in 1909.

By the time the First World War had begun in 1914 the docks at Tilbury were already well established and thriving.

On 10 April 1915 a Royal Naval airship broke loose from its moorings and the pilot fell out into the river mud at West Thurrock. The crew of HMS *Exmouth* threw out grappling hooks and managed to take the airship in tow. There is no mention of what happened to the pilot.

HMS *Exmouth* was a Royal Navy vessel used for training which remained anchored off Grays from 1905 until 1939 and the start of the Second World War.

CHAPTER 3

Declaration of War

Britain declared war on Germany at 2300 hours on 4 August 1914 after the latter's refusal to recognise Belgium's neutrality and remove her troops from the country.

The British Government had earlier given Germany an ultimatum over the matter, but the response was deemed to be unsatisfactory. This led to a meeting between government officials and King George V, after which the following statement was issued by the Home Office:

> *'Owing to the summary rejection by the German Government for assurances that the neutrality of Belgium will be respected, his Majesty's Ambassador to Berlin has received his passports, and his Majesty's Government declared to the German Government that a state of war exists between Great Britain and Germany as from 11pm on 4 August 1914.'*

On 3 August 1914, Sir Edward Grey, the then Foreign Secretary, made an historic speech to the Houses of Parliament on the subject of the growing conflict throughout Europe. Here is what he said:

> *'Last week I stated that we were working for peace, not only for this country, but to preserve the peace of Europe. Today's events move so rapidly that it is exceedingly difficult to state with technical accuracy the actual state of affairs, but it is clear that the peace of Europe cannot be preserved. Russia and Germany, at any rate, have declared war upon each other.*

The French fleet is now in the Mediterranean, and the northern and western coasts of France are absolutely undefended. If a foreign fleet, engaged in a war which France had not sought, and in which she had not been the aggressor, came down the English Channel and bombarded and battered the undefended coasts of France, we could not stand aside with our arms folded. I believe that would be the feeling of this country.

We feel strongly that France is entitled to know, and to know at once, whether or not in the event of attack upon her unprotected northern and western coast she could depend upon British support.

In these compelling circumstances, yesterday afternoon I gave the French ambassador the following statement:

"I am authorised to give an assurance that if the German fleet comes into the Channel or through the North Sea to undertake hostile operations against the French coasts or shipping, the British fleet will give all the protection in its power."

I read that to the House, not as a declaration of war on our part, but as binding us to take aggressive action should that contingency arise.

If France is beaten in a struggle of life and death, beaten to her knees, loses her position as a great power, becomes subordinate to the will and power of one greater than herself, consequences which I do not anticipate, because I am sure that France has the power to defend herself with all the energy and ability and patriotism which she has shown so often, still, if that were to happen, and if Belgium fell under the same dominating influence, and then Holland and then Denmark, then would not Mr Gladstone's words come true, that just opposite to us there would be a common interest against the unmeasured aggrandisement of any power.

We are going to suffer, I am afraid, terribly in this war, whether we are in it or whether we stand aside. Foreign trade is going to stop, not because trade routes are closed, but because there is no trade at the other end.

I do not believe for a moment that at the end of this war, even if we stood aside and remained aside, we should be in a position, to use our force decisively to undo what happened in the course of the war, to prevent the whole of the west of Europe opposite to us, if that had been the result of the war, falling under the domination of a single power, and I am quite sure that our moral position would be such as to have lost us all respect...

The thought is with us always of the suffering and misery entailed, from which no country in Europe will escape, and from which no abdication of neutrality will save us.

I have now put the vital facts before the House, and if, as seems not improbable, we are forced and rapidly forced, to take our stand upon those issues, then I believe, when the country realises what is at stake, what the real issues are, the magnitude of the impending dangers in the West of Europe, which I have endeavoured to describe to the House, we shall be supported throughout, not only by the House of Commons, but by the determination, the resolution, the courage, and the endurance of the whole country.'

Historically the reason that has been proffered as to why Britain declared war on Germany in August 1914, which ultimately lead to the untimely deaths of nearly 1,000 of Thurrock's finest young men, has always been that we were trying to protect Belgium from an aggressor, in the shape of Germany.

Sir Edward Grey's speech contained numerous references about protecting France from the same aggressor and the possibility of maybe having to go to war in her defence. His words could be interpreted as to be more about the justification of a political decision which had already been made, rather than a 'what if' scenario. It has to be remembered, of course, that at no time had England been directly threatened by Germany, yet it was she who declared war and not Germany.

It's almost as if Britain had a desire, in a political sense, to go to war with Germany, but needed a sound reason to do so which wouldn't affect its standing on the world stage. The invasion of Belgium and overtly aggressive intentions towards France, provided Britain with the opportunity she was looking for. It could equally be argued that because of the numerous alliances countries had in place with their friendly neighbours throughout Europe, Britain had no real choice in the matter.

After reading Sir Edward Grey's speech, one is left to ponder the question of what would have happened if Germany had ceded to Britain's demand to remove her troops from Belgium, as it would appear by the tone of the speech that the decision to declare war on Germany had already been taken.

The other confusing element of his speech was the somewhat exaggerated claim, 'we are ready', which was quite clearly not the case. At the outbreak of the First World War Germany already had an experienced army of some 4.5 million men, compared to that of the British Army which numbered only about 80,000.

CHAPTER 4

Timeline of the War

1914

28 June. Archduke Franz Ferdinand, heir to the Austro-Hungarian throne and his pregnant wife Sophie, were assassinated by Gavrilo Princip, a Bosnian-Serb, whilst on a visit to Sarajevo. This act led directly to the outbreak of the First World War.

28 July. Austria-Hungary issued an ultimatum against Serbia, which Serbia failed to comply with in its entirety. Austria-Hungary then declared war on Serbia.

29 July. Austria-Hungary began offensive operations against Serbia by crossing the border and marching to Mitrovitza.

1 August. Germany declares war on Russia after Russia had mobilized both her army and navy. Germany, feeling directly threatened by these actions requested Russia stand down her forces, but having received no response, Germany declared a state of war between the two countries.

3 August. Germany declares war on France. The Schlieffen Plan was drawn up by Germany on the basis that she would be at war with France and Russia at the same time. The plan had been evolving since 1897 because of Germany's certainty that there would be a European war brought about largely because of the political alliances that had been formed throughout those years.

Political frailties were felt both on a national and international level by many countries which led to the signing of military alliances for protection in case of invasion by a hostile neighbour.

Germany believed she could quickly defeat France then attack

Russia before she had been able to mobilise her forces. The plan started to go wrong when Russia mobilised both her army and navy in double quick time. Germany now needed to deal with France quickly, so on the pretence that she felt a French attack was imminent, she declared war on France claiming that she had no option and was acting in self-defence.

Sir Edward Grey, the Foreign Secretary, addresses Parliament on the possibility of war in Europe and whether Britain should intervene.

4 August. Germany declares war on Belgium after her request that her army be allowed to march through Belgium to carry out a surprise attack on France was refused.

Great Britain declares war on Germany. Belgium had requested help from Great Britain after she was invaded by Germany. After Germany's refusal to comply with this request, the British Government declared war on Germany.

President Woodrow Wilson declares the US policy of neutrality concerning any involvement in the war.

7 August. Lord Kitchener, the Secretary of State for War, announces the need for 100,000 men to enlist and join the British Army.

First British troops arrive in France with the British Expeditionary Force (BEF) commanded by Field Marshal Sir John French.

10 August. France declares war on Austria-Hungary.

12 August. Great Britain declares war on Austria-Hungary.

23 August. Japan declares war on Germany. Unlike in the Second World War where she was an enemy, Britain and Japan were allies during the First World War.

Troops from the BEF see action for the first time since hostilities began at the Battle of Mons.

26-30 August. Germany defeated Russia at The Battle of Tannenberg; 50,000 Russian soldiers were either killed or wounded during the fighting, with another 100,000 being captured and taken prisoner.

28 August 28 The British naval victory off Heligoland was the first naval battle of the war. Three German light cruisers and a destroyer were sunk and another three light cruisers were damaged by the British navy.

6-11 September. Battle of the Marne near Paris which sees British and French troops fighting side by side for the first time against the Germans. The German advance on Paris is halted marking the failure of the Schlieffen Plan.

15 October. Fighting begins at the first Battle of Ypres in western Belgium.

31 October. HMS *Hermes* was torpedoed by the German U-Boat, *U-27* off Ruylingen Bank in the Straits of Dover, and sank with the loss of 22 of her crew. Her captain, Charles Lambe survived the attack.

5 November. On 29 October 1914, the Ottoman Empire (Turkey) sided with Germany and helped her in a naval bombardment of Russia. Russia then declared war on Turkey on 2 November 1914 and so Britain and France then followed suit in support of their ally, Russia, and also declared war on the Ottoman Empire.

16 December. Germany carried out a daring naval raid of the north-east coast of England. Shells rained down on West Hartlepool, Scarborough and Whitby, killing 127 civilians with twice that number being injured.

25 December. A Christmas Day truce takes place on the Western Front which sees British and German troops meet in no man's land and exchange pleasantries and cigarettes. Official records show that forty-one British soldiers were killed in action on Christmas Day 1914, so although historically it is depicted as being a day of peace and tranquillity, that's not totally accurate.

1915

19 January. Two German naval Zeppelin airships, Zeppelins L3 and L4 left their base in Germany planning to attack the Humber area of Britain, but were foiled by bad weather. They were forced to switch their attacks to the coastal towns of Norfolk. L3 dropped its bombs on Great Yarmouth, killing two people. Samuel Alfred Smith became the first British civilian to be killed by aerial bombardment. Martha Taylor was the second person killed, with a further three people injured as a result of the attacks.

21 January. The naval battle off Dogger Bank took place between the British Grand Fleet and the German High Seas Fleet. As the British lost no ships and suffered few casualties during the battle, and the Germans lost a ship and most of its crew, the action was considered to be a British victory. Both sides learnt lessons as a result of the encounter with the British and German navies replacing some of their commanders who were thought to have shown poor judgement.

4 February. Germany begins its U-boat campaign of torpedoing and sinking British and Allied shipping.

26 February. Flamethrowers are used by the Germans for the first time during the war, in fighting near Verdun on the Western Front.

15 April. The French use poison gas against the Germans for the first time in fighting near Verdun.

22 April. The Second Battle of Ypres takes place, where the Germans use chlorine gas against the French.

25 April. Allied forces including those from Australia, France and Britain, land in Gallipoli.

7 May. The RMS *Lusitania*, an ocean-going passenger liner, was on her way from New York to Liverpool when she was torpedoed by a German submarine and sunk 11 miles off the south coast of Ireland; 1,198 passengers and crew were killed, including 128 US citizens. In firing on a non-military ship without warning, the Germans had breached the international laws known as the Cruiser Rules. Germany had reasons for treating the *Lusitania* as a naval vessel, in part because she was carrying munitions for the British war effort, which was also a breach of the Cruiser Rules. The sinking caused a storm of protest in the United States and was a major influence on their decision to eventually declare war on Germany in 1917.

31 May. The first German Zeppelin raid took place on London, resulting in the deaths of seven civilians.

6 August. An Allied amphibious landing takes place at Suvla Bay, as part of the August offensive, the final British attempt to break the deadlock of the Battle for Gallipoli. The landing was intended to support a breakout from the Anzac sector, five miles to the south. Despite facing light opposition, the landing at Suvla Bay was mismanaged from the outset and quickly reached the same stalemate which prevailed on the Anzac and Helles fronts.

15 August. After a week of indecision and inactivity, the British commander at Suvla, Lieutenant General Sir Frederick Stopford was dismissed. His performance in command was deemed to have been one of the most incompetent feats of generalship of the First World War.

8 September. German Zeppelin raid on London. Twenty people were killed and another eighty-six were injured. This was a major change of tactics on behalf of the Germans as previously Kaiser Wilhelm had given express orders that there were to be no attacks on London itself owing to his concern for the British Royal family to whom he was related.

5 October. Allied forces land at Salonika at the behest of the Greek Prime Minister, Eleftherios Venizelos. The French commander, General Maurice Sarrail and General George Milne, the leader of the British troops, turned Salonika and its surrounds into an entrenched zone with a trench-system similar to that on the Western Front.

13 October. A German Zeppelin raid on London and the east coast of England leaves fifty-six dead and another 114 injured.

15 December. Sir Douglas Haig replaced Sir John French as British commander-in-chief in France.

1916

8 January. The end of evacuation of British troops from the Gallipoli Peninsula. The campaign was considered to be a major military failure for the allied forces.

21 February. Battle of Verdun begins and continued until 18 December 1916. It was fought by French and German armies.

24 April. The Irish rebellion, also known as the Easter Rising, began and lasted for six days. Irish Republicans by their actions, attempted to end British rule in Ireland and establish an independent Irish Republic.

29 April. Fall of Kut. An 8,000 strong British/Indian Army had held off the might of the Ottoman Army since 7 December 1915.

24 May. The British Government passed the Military Service Act 1916, which specified that single men aged between 18 and 41 years were liable to be called up for military service.

31 May. The Battle of Jutland, off the coast of Jutland in Denmark. The Allies lost fourteen ships and over 6,000 men whilst the Germans lost eleven ships and 2,500 men.

5 June. Loss at sea of Lord Kitchener and staff when the warship, HMS *Hampshire*, which was taking him to negotiations in Russia hit a German mine and sank.

1 July. The first day of the Battle of Somme, with 58,000 casualties including almost 19,000 killed, was the worst ever suffered by the British Army. The campaign lasted until November 1916. Over 1,000,000 men from both sides were either killed or wounded in the five months that it lasted.

29 August. Paul von Hindenburg appointed Chief of German Staff.

3 September. German Zeppelin brought down in Cuffley, Hertfordshire.

23-24 September. Two German Zeppelins, L32 and L33, were brought down in Great Burstead and Little Wigborough in Essex.

5 December. British Prime Minister Asquith resigns to be replaced by David Lloyd George.

1917

31 January. Germany announces unrestricted submarine warfare.

24 February. British forces take Kut.

8 March. Russian Revolution begins.

6 April. America finally declares war on Germany.

7-14 June. British victory at Battle of Messines Ridge which began when 19 mines were detonated beneath the German lines.

13 June. Daylight raid on London by German Gotha bombers results in 157 deaths and 432 wounded civilians.

16 June. The German Zeppelin L48 was brought down in Suffolk by four British aircraft.

26 June. The first American troops arrive in France

24 September - 4 October. After being forced to stop their day time raids on England mainly due to improved British air defences, there followed a week of night raids on London by German aircraft.

6 November. After three months of fighting in appalling conditions British and Canadian troops capture the village of Passchendaele ending the Third Battle of Ypres.

7 November. The Russian General Staff surrender to Bolshevik Forces during the Russian Revolution.

1918

2 March. Russian–German peace treaty signed at Brest-Litovsk.

21 March. Start of German Spring Offensive, the *Kaiserschlact*, Germany's last attempt to win the war.

19 May. The last German aeroplane raid takes place on London.

5 August. The last German Zeppelin raid takes place on England.

8 August. The British and Allied forces' Hundred Days Offensive begins on a 20-mile front, east of Amiens.

31 August. The Australian Army takes Mont Saint-Quentin and then Peronne.

18 September - 17 October. The Allies break through Germany's Hindenburg Line.

26 September. Start of the Meuse-Argonne Offensive, involving over one million American soldiers.

27 October. Germany announces that she wants proposals from the Allies for an armistice.

30 October. The Ottoman Empire surrenders and signs an armistice.

30 October. Austria surrenders and also signs an armistice.

9 November. The German emperor, Kaiser Wilhelm II abdicates.

11 November. Mons occupied at dawn. Armistice signed at 5am and hostilities ceased at 11am.

CHAPTER 5

Thurrock's First Casualty of the War

Whilst researching this book we came across *Thurrock 1914 – 1918, The Great War* by Roger Reynolds. The book showed that Thurrock's first casualty of the Great War was Private James Allen, of the Queen's Own (Royal West Kent Regiment) and that he was only 19 years of age at the time of his death on 23 August 1914, just a matter of days into the war. His family lived at Maidstone Place in Grays.

We could not recall having seen his name on any of the district's war memorials, although that could have simply been down to a clerical oversight or perhaps his name had been included on another town's memorial.

We then checked the website of the Commonwealth War Graves Commission (CWGC) to see if they had any information. Having entered the name James Allen, the system came up with 294 possible matches, but not one of them had died on 23 August 1914. When we added the name of the regiment Private James Allen served with, the Queen's Own (Royal West Kent Regiment), this came up with only one possible, but his name was John Allen and he died on 17 July 1917.

We then looked at the 1911 Census on Ancestry.co.uk and found a James Allen, aged 17, at 8 Maidstone Place, Grays in Essex. He lived with his mother, Ellen Grimwade, his stepfather, William James Grimwade, a dock labourer, one would imagine at the nearby Tilbury Docks, and two sisters, Gladys (9) and Ellen (4). Prior to the war James's occupation was farm labourer.

In the 1901 census and James, William and Ellen, are shown with the surname Grimwood and not Grimwade which on the hand written copy, is clearly Grimwood. There were also two other siblings, Florie Allen (10) and William Allen (8). At this time they were living at 17 George Street, Grays in Essex.

We then looked at the military records on Ancestry.co.uk and checked for James Allen – and bingo, we found him! This was where it really started to become interesting. We first looked at his Attestation papers, which showed he had enlisted in the Army before the war had even started, on 28 January 1913. He signed on for twelve years; seven years serving with the colours and a further five years on the reserve. His service number was 10079.

It is apparent from looking at the papers from James Allen's military record, that they had been partly damaged, possibly from fire, but what was there was more than legible. It showed that he was a small man, 5 feet 3 inches in height and weighing 117lbs or eight and a half stone. He had a 35-inch chest with a 4-inch expansion, a fresh complexion, light blue eyes and brown hair.

The oath of allegiance which he swore at his attestation was as follows:

'I, James Allen do make oath, that I will be faithful and bear true allegiance to his Majesty, King George the Fifth, his heirs and successors, and that I will, as in duty bound, honestly and faithfully defend his Majesty, his heirs and successors, in person, crown and dignity against all enemies, and will observe and obey all orders of his Majesty, his heirs and successors, and of the General and officers set over me. So help me God.'

We checked the British Army First World War medal rolls index cards for James Allen, and much to our surprise it showed that he had been awarded the 1914 Star, the British War Medal and the Victory Medal. It would not have been possible for him to have been awarded the last two medals if he had died on 23 August 1914.

We searched through the documents which were held in his military service record and discovered that not only did Private James Allen not die on 23 August 1914, he survived the war, not being fully discharged from the army until 5 February 1920.

The confusion had arisen because on 23 August 1914 James Allen wasn't killed during the fighting in and around Mons, but was captured by the Germans and spent the rest of the war in captivity at Parchim prisoner of war camp in north-east Germany. The camp at Parchim was built on what had once been a German cavalry drill ground, which was surrounded by pinewoods in an enclosure that was 3 miles in circumference. It was 3 miles from the nearby railway station and at times there were up to 45,000 men detained there.

James Allen was a prisoner of war for a total of four years and 132 days, having been captured just nine days after having arrived in France as part of the British Expeditionary Force. He was eventually repatriated to Britain on 2 January 1919 but it would still be another year before he was finally discharged from the army, on 5 February 1920.

The same book also showed that Thurrock's second casualty of the war was Private William Jiggens, but the discovery that Private James Allen hadn't in fact been killed, meant that he was now Thurrock's first casualty of the war.

His full name was William Francis Jiggens (10156), a 19-year-old private in the 2nd Battalion of the Essex Regiment. He was killed on 26 August 1914 whilst serving in France and is commemorated on the La Ferté-Sous-Jouarre War Memorial in the Seine-et-Marne region of France. His name has also been included on the Corringham Church Plaque as well as the Stanford-le-Hope War Memorial where it is spelt incorrectly as 'Jiggins'.

The Commonwealth War Graves Commission memorial at La Ferté-sous-Jouarre commemorates 3,740 officers and men of the British Expeditionary Force (BEF) who fell at the Battles of Mons, Le Cateau, the Marne and the Aisne between the end of August and early October 1914 and who have no known graves.

Designed by George H. Goldsmith, a decorated veteran of the Western Front, it was unveiled by Sir William Pulteney on 4 November 1928 who had commanded the III Corps of the British Expeditionary Force in 1914.

By the time the Commonwealth War Graves Commission collated their records in the early 1920s, William Francis Jiggens' mother, Mary Warren, was living at 3 Shell Cottages, Shell Haven, Stanford-Le-Hope, Essex.

In the 1911 Census the family were at 13 Grove Road, Stanford-le-Hope, Essex. Alfred James Warren and Mary Warren had been married for nine years by 1911, meaning that all four of Mary's children had been born to her previous husband. The oldest child was Samuel Peter Jiggens (19), then Amy Susan Jiggens (17), William Francis Jiggens (16) and Henry James Jiggens (14).

On the 1901 Census Mary Jiggens is shown as a widow who made her living as a 'char woman'. Along with her four children she lived at number 176 King Street, Stanford-le-Hope, Essex.

CHAPTER 6

Augusto Alfredo Roggen – A Spy

On 30 May 1915 Augusto Alfredo Roggen, a Uruguayan who was born in Montevideo in 1881, arrived at Tilbury docks on board the SS *Batavia*, which had sailed from Rotterdam in Holland.

He then made his way up to Edinburgh, under the pretence of being a farmer, arriving there on 5 June where he booked into the Carlton Hotel. Whilst in the capitol he did some sightseeing, went on a day trip to the Trossachs and registered with the local police, which was a wartime requirement for foreign nationals visiting and travelling around Great Britain.

Whilst in Edinburgh he did what most tourists would do and sent a couple of postcards. There were addressed to somebody by the name of H. Flores at an address in Rotterdam, Holland. Unfortunately for Augusto the address to which he had sent the postcards was well known to the British Security Services, which not surprisingly then brought him to their close attention. The details on the postcards were copied before they were forwarded on to the address in Holland. At the time the German Consul in Rotterdam played an active part in all of their country's intelligence operations, so it is inconceivable to think that Augusto wasn't working for them.

Augusto arrived at the Tarbet Hotel on 9 June and within five hours he was arrested during a police raid on his room. There the police found a loaded Browning revolver, with fifty rounds of ammunition, some invisible ink, a map of the area, which included Loch Long, and a list of contacts.

His real reason for travelling to Great Britain was to observe and if possible, photograph the work that was going on at Loch Long at the Arrochar Torpedo range which had been opened in 1912.

He was taken to London by Police Superintendent John Wright where on arrival he was handed over to Detective Inspector Edmund Buckley from the Metropolitan Police's Special Branch department. When interviewed he offered no defence to the allegations of spying that had been made against him. At his subsequent trial at the Middlesex Guildhall in Westminster, on 20 August he was found guilty and sentenced to death by firing squad. The sentence was carried out at the Tower of London at 0600 hours on 17 September 1915, by members of the 3rd Battalion of the Scots Guards. He was 34 years old.

Luckily for the British authorities, but unluckily for Augusto, he was not that good a spy and his purpose for being in Scotland was all too easily ascertained.

Roggen was one of eleven German spies who were captured and executed at the Tower of London during the First World War on charges brought under the Defence of the Realm Act (DORA).

Once sentenced to death by the British authorities, it was the Uruguayan and not the German government which made a request for clemency for Augusto, even though he was undoubtedly working and spying for Germany when he was captured.

The responsibility for intelligence gathering and operations within the German military machine during the First World War lay with their Naval Intelligence section, with which Augusto would have been liaising and who would have sent him on the mission to Scotland which cost him his life.

Augusto had two brothers, Federico and Emilio. Their mother was Uruguayan and their father, although a naturalised Uruguayan, was German by birth.

CHAPTER 7

Gunther Plüschow – Escaped PoW

Gunther Plüschow was a German naval officer and pilot who was being held as a prisoner of war at Donnington Hall PoW camp in Leicestershire when he escaped on 4 July 1915. He arrived in Germany by train on 13 July 1915 and for his extraordinary exploits of heroism and determination, was awarded the Iron Cross, First Class, by Kaiser Wilhelm II.

Donnington Hall was, and still, is a breathtaking location, in a 1,100 acre estate in Castle Donnington. At the beginning of the First World War, it was requisitioned by the British Government and turned into a prisoner of war camp for captured German officers. Gunther Plüschow was one of the many who were held

Gunthur Pluschow.

there. He found fame and notoriety when he became the only German prisoner of war to escape from Britain and make it back home to Germany.

When the First World War began in August 1914, Lieutenant Plüschow as he was then, was stationed at the East Asian Naval station at Tsingtau, which was a German colony in China. On 23 August 1914 after Japan had declared war on Germany, her forces alongside those from Britain, besieged the German colony at Tsingtau after she had refused Japanese requests to evacuate her military presence there.

On 6 November 1914 Plüschow was ordered to fly a number of official despatches and other important documents back to Germany. After he had flown for about 160 miles, he crashed into a paddy field; whether he had run out of fuel or had engine trouble is not known. However, fortune shone upon him and he escaped unscathed from the crash. After setting fire to his Taube aircraft to ensure it didn't fall into 'enemy hands' he set off on the long and arduous journey back home to Germany on foot. He had set himself a formidable task.

His starting point was Daschou. From there he made his way to Nanking, where he arrived by river in a Chinese junk. From there he took a train to Shanghai, and once there was provided with documents from a German diplomat who he knew from Berlin, which purported to show him as a Swiss national. He was also provided with money and a ticket on a ship which was sailing to San Francisco in America, travelling via Nagasaki and Honolulu.

His resourcefulness took him across America eventually arriving in New York City. There he met a friend from Berlin who got him on a ship bound for Italy which sailed on 30 January 1915. Because of bad weather the ship was unable to reach Italy and instead it had to land in Gibraltar where he was immediately arrested by the British authorities as an enemy alien when they discovered his true identity.

He arrived at Donnington Hall PoW camp on 1 July 1915 only to escape three days later during a heavy storm. He had no intention of comfortably seeing out the war in his new-found opulent surroundings. From Donnington he made his way to London where he overheard a conversation on a bus about a ship that sailed daily from Tilbury Docks to Flushing in Holland. He took a train to Tilbury where he looked for a ship flying the Dutch colours which would help to get him back to Germany. He still had a lot of work to do once he spotted the ship. He had to somehow get on board it and that was going to be no mean feat.

After waiting nearly all day by the water's edge at Tilbury, a Dutch vessel, the *Mecklenberg*, sailed passed him as he sat amongst the long grass of the riverbank. His excitement was tempered by the realisation that he couldn't be certain where the ship would be sailing to, or even if it was the ship he had overheard the two men talking about on the

London bus. For all he knew it could be sailing across the Atlantic to America.

After failing to get on board the *Mecklenberg* two nights on the run, he was left feeling cold, tired and hungry and wondering if he was actually going to be able to make good his escape. During the day he had to hide up on the riverbank hoping that he wasn't going to be discovered by the British soldiers who regularly patrolled the docks area.

Luck and good fortune were on his side again when he saw another Dutch vessel, the *Princess Juliana*, moored nearby. Once again he had no idea where she was sailing to so he had to make a decision one way or the other. He decided to go for it and that evening, under the cover of darkness, he floated a small boat out to the *Princess Juliana*, climbed up the side of the ship and hid in one of the lifeboats. The following day he arrived in

Pluschow with iron cross.

Flushing in neutral Holland. At last he was a free man. Next stop Germany.

His feat was remarkable by anybody's standards. After nearly making it home the first time all the way from China, he was only thwarted at the last step of the journey by an act of God which placed him in the hands of the British at Gibraltar. He managed to escape once again and this time he successfully made it all the way back home to Germany.

As well as being awarded the Iron Cross, he was promoted to the rank of Kapitänleutnant and given command of the German naval base at Libau (Liepāja) in occupied Latvia. He survived the war and died in a plane crash in Argentina on 28 January 1931, aged 45. He was survived by his wife and his son Guntolf.

Reformatory School Ship
Cornwall – Purfleet

The idea for Reformatory Ships had first come about in 1859 as a result of an idea from Sir George Henry Chambers, who wanted to help deal with what seemed to be an ever increasing problem in society. Through a combination of single mothers who had lost husbands, orphaned children or dysfunctional families who could ill afford to fend for themselves, some young men made wrong decisions, got in with the wrong crowd and became a burden on society.

It was hoped that the Reformatory Ships would teach these young men about discipline, friendship and a feeling of wellbeing which would ultimately provide them with the skills and opportunity to lead useful and worthwhile lives. Most boys who spent time on the ships were paupers and for most it was a much better option than stagnating in a workhouse.

One such ship had been moored off Purfleet since 1868; it was named the *Cornwall* and had first been launched in 1815 as HMS *Wellesley*.

On 30 August 1915, Edward Francis Lane, the *Cornwall*'s training officer was transferring a group of boys from shore to the ship in a small cutter (*Alert*). There were sixteen boys on board, aged between 14 and 18, when it was in collision with the *Empress* tug boat, under the command of Sergeant Major Black of the Royal Engineers. The training officer and all sixteen of the boys were unfortunately killed in the accident.

The *Cornwall* had room for 240 boys at any one time. All seventeen of those who died were buried on 8 September 1915.

The names of the sixteen boys are:

Ernest BEARSLY (17)
Thomas LEADER (17)
Frederick BURNISTON (16)
Henry LEE (16)
James CHURCH (16)
Cyril MANN (14)
Charles CLEWS (16)
Richard MILLARD (17)
William EVANS (16)
William ROWLANDS (18)
Charles GIPP (14)
William SMITH (15)
William HILLYER (16)
Walter TOWNSEND (16)
Henry JESSOP (13)
Arthur YOUNG (14)

All the victims were buried in a communal plot at St Clement's Church in West Thurrock. Over 3,000 local friends and relatives attended the ceremony. In more recent times the same church was made famous when it was used in the film *Four Weddings and a Funeral*.

CHAPTER 9

L15 Zeppelin – Shot Down 31 March 1916

At 9:45pm on the evening of 31 March 1916, the German Zeppelin, L15 received a direct hit from ground-based anti-aircraft batteries that were operating in the area at the time. Not surprisingly, more than one of the batteries claimed to have been the one responsible for hitting the Zeppelin and for its ultimate demise. Some reports claim it was the battery at Purfleet that was the first to hit the L15, others claim it was the one at Tilbury Fort that was responsible for causing the initial damage.

The crew of the Zeppelin tried their best to maintain height by throwing overboard anything they could from the stricken airship, but the damage to the airship was too great. As it continued its unavoidable descent it was attacked by Second Lieutenant Alfred de Bathe Brandon of the Royal Flying Corps, who was stationed at Hainault Farm in Essex. In his BE2c Brandon climbed above L15 and tried to destroy it by dropping incendiary bombs and Ranken darts onto the top of the hull, but without success.

Regardless of which battery actually fired the damaging salvo, what is unarguable is that the Zeppelin suffered damage to four of its gas cells and started to lose height and subsequently crashed into the sea off of Margate close to the Kentish Knock Lightship at 00:15am on 1 April 1916.

Of the crew of sixteen, fifteen survived. Unfortunately the other

Alfred de Bathe Brandon's aircraft.

L-15 Zeppelin.

crew member, Willy Albrecht, was drowned when the Zeppelin crashed into the sea. The surviving members of the crew were rescued by the armed trawler *Olivine* and then transferred to HMS *Vulture*.

The remains of L15 were then taken under tow but the airship broke up off Westgate and only small sections of it were eventually hauled ashore.

Otto Kuhne was somewhat of a character. Not only did he survive the First World War, but also survived the Second World War. He stayed in the German Navy until May 1935 when at the age of 46 he became a major in the German Luftwaffe. By the end of the war he was a general in charge of signals for the Luftwaffe in Norway. He was captured in May 1945 and handed over to the British authorities who detained him in PoW camps, until 10 October 1947, when he returned to his native country.

He died on 19 March 1987 in Gottmadingen-Bietigheim in German, less than three months away from his 100th birthday.

Sir Charles Wakefield, Lord Mayor of London in 1916, had promised a significant monetary reward for the first anti-aircraft gun crew to shoot down a Zeppelin. In the aftermath of the event, so many anti-aircraft crews and searchlight batteries claimed to have been the ones who had initially struck the L15 that some 300, 8-carat gold medals were issued to various members of the gun crews and searchlight batteries involved.

Second Lieutenant Alfred de Bathe Brandon attacked numerous German Zeppelins during their raids on eastern England throughout 1916 and, although he has been credited with the destruction of the L15 Zeppelin, the evidence to confirm that is far from being clear.

Whether his attack on the stricken airship on the night of 31 March 1916 caused it to crash in the sea or whether anti-aircraft fire from British ground batteries was wholly or partly responsible has long been the subject of

Captain Joachim Breithaupt and Oberlieutnant Otto Kuhne.

controversy. But his assault on L-15, at 9,000 feet while being subjected to enemy machine-gun fire, won him a Distinguished Service Order (DSO), making him the first New Zealander to win that award.

After the war he returned to his native New Zealand, quit the military and returned to his pre-war job of practising law. Like a lot of men of his generation he didn't really speak much about his wartime exploits until 1932.

The captain of the L15 Zeppelin, Kapitanleutnant Joachim Breithaupt, gave a lecture about the evening of the 31 March 1916 which was recorded in the BBC publication *The Listener* on 8 June 1932. He said: *'For a long time a flyer accompanied us but he did not manage to attain our height and lost us.'*

This resulted in Brandon feeling the need to give his account of the same event in some detail:

> *'I was always of the opinion that I brought the L15 down. Officially the guns were credited with it. I got the credit publicly and was decorated for dropping bombs on it.*
>
> *The reason why the gunners got the credit was, it would appear, that the crew of the Zeppelin had said that they had been hit by gunfire. As against this the barman at Donnington Hall reported that German officers interned there had admitted that it was the airman that had got them.*
>
> *However in 1932 Kapitain Leutnant Breihaupt, who actually was the commander of the L15 when it was brought down, gave a broadcast lecture which was recorded in the BBC official paper,* The Listener, *of the 8th June, and in this lecture he not only said he was hit by gunfire, but he went much further, he said: "For a long time a flyer accompanied us but he did not manage to attain our height and lost us."*
>
> *If this evidence were accurate (and coming from the actual Captain of the ship it would appear to be so) it would mean:*
>
> *(1) That the Zeppelin had been brought down by gunfire.*
>
> *(2) That I had gained kudos and a decoration by false pretence because my evidence was that I had passed over the Zeppelin and had dropped bombs (or to be more accurate, high explosive Rankin Darts) but did not know definitely whether they had taken effect or not.*

*As a result of my enquiries following the above mentioned
lecture I am satisfied that the Zeppelin was not hit by gunfire,
and further that she was actually brought down by myself.*

*My conclusions are based on the following evidence and
deductions...'*

Brandon goes on to explain that some of the captured officers admitted
to the barman at Donnington Hall that *'the airman had got them'*. The
barman, thought to be a British intelligence officer, sent a telegram to
the air ministry reporting the conversation but it arrived too late to be
included in the official report.

Brandon describes what happened that night:

*'In a fraction of a split second I let off a nest of three bombs.
These apparently did not explode probably because I was under
the requisite height of 500 feet from the Zeppelin...*

*The aeroplane passed over the Zeppelin from the left hand
side and dropped three bombs on the ship and it was damaged
high up and on the left hand side and three ballonets were
punctured, the crew try to show that they were brought down by
gunfire but in point of fact their evidence is erroneous,
contradictory, and in one important point definitely misleading.
It is clear therefore from this aspect of the case that it was the
aeroplane that was successful and not the guns.'*

In a letter sent to Brandon by Breithaupt in 1932 the German officer
said that after the Zeppelin was hit *'an aeroplane accompanied us for
a considerable distance'*. Brandon deduces from the letter's content
that Breithaupt did not witness his first attack from above as he would
have been in his usual place in the airship's gondola. He adds:

*'Whilst acknowledging the invaluable co-operation of both the
guns and the searchlights it is submitted that ... there is really
no satisfactory evidence in favour of the guns whilst that in
favour of the aeroplane is overwhelming.*

Although the Broadcast Lecture as recorded in The Listener
*places me in a very unsavoury position I have no feeling against
the gallant Captain and crew of the Zeppelin. When I first read*

the lecture I saw nothing but a fiery red, but I accept the statement of Kapitanleutnant Breithaupt when he says that he wishes he had my evidence before he gave the lecture.'

Brandon clearly felt affronted by the words of Breithaupt and members of his crew. He was in a difficult position; if he didn't defend himself against what others might see as an inference that he had obtained his DSO by falsehoods, the inference might well be seen by others to be fact.

His riposte did appear to contain a lot of assumptions and guesswork which he then proffered as fact. But why Breithaupt would lie about what happened is equally baffling, especially as the events had taken place sixteen years earlier.

It would appear that at least one of the anti-aircraft ground based batteries hit L15 with their raking gunfire high up in the dark night sky; which one, cannot be ascertained all these years later. It might have been the crews from Tilbury Fort, it could have also been those stationed at nearby Purfleet. What is also not known is what if any subsequent damage was caused to L15 by their bullets.

Brandon married Ada Mabel Perry at the Cathedral Church of St Paul, Wellington on 2 January 1942. He was 58 years of age and Ada was 38. They had one son called Peter de Bathe Brandon.

Alfred de Bathe Brandon MC DSO MID died on 19 June 1974. He was 90 years of age.

CHAPTER 10

The Battle of the Somme 1916

The first day of the Battle of the Somme, 1 July 1916, was a beautiful sunny day with clear blue skies and just a hint of mist as the sun came up. At 7.30am whistles were blown up and down the front line trenches. After a week of near continuous artillery bombardment of the German positions, this was the long awaited signal for British troops to climb out of their trenches and advance towards their enemy in the mistaken belief that most, if not all of them, had already been killed.

No sooner had they taken their first few steps than they were cut down by savage and intense German machine-gun fire, which quickly decimated their numbers. There was no turning back, no stopping to render assistance to the man next to them who had just fallen, the victim of a German bullet. It was onwards as fast as they could, hoping that they wouldn't be the next to die.

By the end of that first day some 60,000 British soldiers had become casualties, almost 20,000 of whom had been killed. This remains largest loss in a single day in British military history.

The earlier clear blue skies and the peace and tranquillity of the Somme had been replaced with a mixture of death and mayhem as a generation of brave young men had been slaughtered.

And that was just the first day. The Somme campaign ground on until November weather brought it to a close. By then the Allies had advanced about 5 miles at a cost of around 420,000 British and Commonwealth casualties.

CHAPTER 11

Private Frederick Walter (de) Vere

On a visit to Tilbury Fort I discovered a military display in one of the houses which was originally part of the officers' quarters. The display covered both wars and included some very interesting items. With the kind permission of English Heritage, which looks after the Fort, they are related here.

Private 32019 Frederick Walter De Vere was a member of the 11th section, 8th Platoon, X Company of the 1st Battalion, the Essex Regiment. During the First World War he was wounded, captured and imprisoned in Limburg in Germany.

Frederick attested on 18 November 1915 and was immediately placed on the army reserve list. It would be another four months before he would be mobilized and called up to the colours on 27 March 1916. There followed six months of intense training at different locations around the UK as he was prepared for deployment to one of the theatres of war. On 4 January 1917 he landed in France and the following month on 12 February 1917 he was posted to the 1st Battalion the Essex Regiment.

On 14 April 1917 he was officially listed as missing in action. Initially it wasn't known what had happened to him. Nobody knew if he had been wounded, killed, drowned in a bomb crater or blown to pieces by an exploding artillery shell. Such was the confusion surrounding the circumstances of his disappearance that it wasn't until 10 May 1917 that his family were informed back home in England.

On 26 June 1917 it was officially confirmed by the German authorities that Frederick had been captured, taken prisoner and sent to Limburg prisoner of war camp in Germany. He would spend the next eighteen months there before being released after the war on 2 December 1918. He arrived back in England three days later and was discharged from the Army on 17 March 1919 for 'being no longer fit for war service' because of a lung complaint.

Prior to being captured and whilst incarcerated in Limburg as a prisoner of war, he wrote a series of letters home to his family in Ramsden Heath, near Billericay, Essex.

In the 1911 Census he is shown as Frederick Vere. He was 14 years of age at the time, but it doesn't show whether he was at school or already out working, which was normal for boys of such an age back then. The obvious thing to say here would be that it's not the same person, but having researched the 1911 Census, we would suggest that it is, but for some reason he or somebody else has changed his name ever so slightly. Frederick's father's name was Walter and his mother was Esther.

On his attestation document his name is clearly shown as Frederick Walter Vere.

There are five letters to look at, two before he was captured and three when he was a prisoner of war.

The first one is dated 16 November 1916 and was sent from Felixstowe in Suffolk whilst undergoing basic training before being sent out to France.

'In bayonet fighting we bring the rifle up and hold it against our chest holding it until our arms feel as if they are going to break. Then we get the word "At the throat. Point". We rush forward, drive our bayonet home, grip the top of the rifle and at the same time put our foot on the dummy and withdraw the bayonet, then rush on and over another deep trench, stab another dummy, climb up the other side, double around the trench and repeat the above motions again and again. My word, it does make me feel tired.

We had some very fat meat, a few haricot beans and bread today. You wouldn't believe how hungry I get down here.

Your loving Fred'

It doesn't say who the letter was addressed to but one would assume it was sent his mother, Esther.

The second letter is dated 28 January 1917. He has by now moved on from his basic training and is now in France. It has to be remembered that such letters were censored so that they didn't reveal locations or anything that could be construed as negative to national morale. This letter is addressed to both his mother and father and is a simple list of items he has been received in a parcel from Sophie who, it is assumed, is either his girlfriend or fiancée.

> 'Dearest Mum and Dad,
> We are going up the line tomorrow.
> I had a lovely parcel from Sophie:
> A sultana cake.
> A dozen oxo cubes.
> A tin of fresh butter.
> A shaving brush.
> A shaving kit wallet.
> Trench paste.
> Trench powder for the body.
> Cough cure – beastly tasting.
> A large slab of toffee.
> Paper and envelopes.
> An astringent pencil for cuts and bruises.
> Two newspapers.
> And lastly she sent me her . . . a lovely little thing.
> Your loving son,
> Fred

The next letter is dated 7 March 1917 and sent from France.

> 'Ever since I left the trenches, when I take a long breath I have a long sharp pain go through my side just above the hip. I do not think it is fancy because the doctor actually gave me "light duty" and I was to have had my side painted but they had no stuff to do it with, so I had four rotten tablets to be taken every two hours. I expect that is the usual remedy out here.
> I have received your lovely cake dear Mum. The eggs were a

treat. I know you must have denied yourself a lot to send it considering the price of things just now.

Did you see the pictures in the papers of the Somme front dated 27 Feb? If so I assure you it is a good photo!

I was sorry to hear brother Ted was in the Army. I feel sorry for him. Has he been out here?

Well, good-bye dear.

I remain your loving son, Fred.'

Interestingly, having searched through the 1911 Census for Fred, he was an only child, so we are uncertain as to who the 'Ted' is that he refers to in his letter.

There is no record of a Ted or Edward Vere or de Vere on the CWGC website and nor was there anybody of either name shown on the medal roll listings for the First World War.

A short time after had had been injured and captured at the Battle of Monchy-le-Preux he wrote his first letter as a prisoner of war. The letter was dated 21 April 1917 and would appear to have been written to his father.

'It was at the close of the battle that I was hit by shrapnel. I got one piece in the left arm above the elbow, and two smaller holes in my right leg just above the knee. They are healing fast.

I am allowed to write two letter and four cards in a month. I have to write big and plain so that it can be censored easily. I think our pay goes on the same as I am wounded.

Can you send me a loaf of bread and a bit of margarine or jam. The quickest way is through the Red Cross, but do not trouble mother if you cannot.

My belongings are lost. I was lucky enough to have five francs in my pocket and changed it for four marks to buy this paper.

Can you send me the list of casualties in the 1st Essex on 14 April. I should like to know who got back, not many I'm afraid.

I remain your loving son. Fred.'

It was interesting to note that he had written this letter only to his father Walter, appearing not wanting to worry his mother with such trivialities as sending a loaf of bread and some margarine, although it would be interesting to see what state such items would still be in on their arrival in Germany.

The fighting that Fred refers to in his letter was the Battle of Monchy-le-Preux, which is a village about 7 kilometres south-east of Arras.

The Arras offensive saw British and Canadian Forces attack along a 22 kilometre front. The Newfoundland Regiment, commanded by the highly decorated Lieutenant Colonel James Forbes-Robertson VC DSO and Bar MC, were to attack an enemy objective known as Infantry Hill, with the assistance of the 1st Battalion of the Essex Regiment.

The attack began with an Allied artillery bombardment of the German defensive positions on 14 April 1917. This was the signal for both battalions to begin their attack, but the bombardment had been ineffective, allowing the Germans to mount a counter-attack which resulted in the British and Canadians suffering heavy casualties. By 9am on the first day of the battle, those attackers not killed or wounded, were left with no option but to surrender.

The enemy continued their counter attack, which was such a success that they managed to capture the trenches from which the British and Canadians had launched their original attack earlier in the day.

Lieutenant Colonel Forbes-Robertson and a small number of his men made their way to the outskirts of the village of Monchy-le-Preux, where they set up a defensive position in a shallow ditch and managed to hold off the Germans for eleven hours before being relieved under the cover of darkness. Forbes-Robertson had sent a runner to the rear to inform British officers of the situation. This resulted in men of the Hampshire Regiment being sent forward as support to relieve their beleaguered and exhausted comrades. An artillery bombardment also commenced onto the German positions, which helped to stop them from advancing any further. Sadly this also led to the death by friendly fire of a number of men from the Newfoundland Regiment who were still lying wounded in no man's land.

The Newfoundland Regiment sustained 460 casualties on that first day; 166 of whom were killed or who died of their wounds, with 141 wounded and a further 153 taken prisoner. The 1st Battalion, the Essex Regiment, suffered 602 casualties, 400 of whom were also taken prisoner.

Tactically this was not a total Britsih success, as the decision, possibly because of poor intelligence, to send such a relatively small number of men in to an attack across such a wide front and against much larger German forces, proved very costly. Thankfully the situation was recovered in time, which went some way to assuring an Allied victory at the Battle of Arras.

The last letter is one that was sent on 5 October 1917 from Limburg Prisoner of War camp in Germany where Fred was being held. It was sent to his girlfriend, Sophie, in response to a letter she had sent to him.

> 'Dear Sophie,
>
> How pleased I was to hear from you dear.... The other night I was sick and my head was bad all night long.
>
> When I went 'over the top' in April I was under very heavy fire especially machine gun and artillery from 5.30am to 9.30am and up until 9 o'clock I was advancing, so dear, you can just imagine what a strain it is on one's nerves. Try to imagine yourself walking to work and everybody, all your friends, falling dead and wounded under such fire.
>
> A number of shells fell one after another within a couple of yards of me and I think I was stunned for a bit. Anyway that was the cause of this head trouble. My head has never been right since. But still, dearest, it is nothing to mention.
>
> Well, my dearest. God will take care of you and keep you from all harm, until that long looked for day when we shall give that long postponed kiss.
>
> So good-bye my darling.
>
> I remain your very loving Fred.'

Limburg PoW camp catered for up to 12,000 prisoners and was just one of up to 300 which Germany had spread throughout the country. By October 1918 Germany was responsible for 2,415,000 Allied prisoners of war. This must have presented a logistical nightmare. Not only did they have to house and look after all of these prisoners in a humanitarian way, but they had to feed them as well as have enough soldiers to guard them, which was a drain on their resources that could have been better employed serving on the Western Front.

CHAPTER 12

Thurrock Through the Eyes of the Press

The *Essex Newsman* was a weekly newspaper which was in publication for eighty-nine years from 1870 until 1959. It contained weekly news from all across the county of Essex.

Four days after the declaration of war the *Essex Newsman* printed their first newspaper of the war. Some of the articles it contained not only gave a flavour of the war, but what life was like back home.

Below are a selection of articles from that first wartime edition.

At the top of the front page immediately under the name of the newspaper and the date, was the following paragraph with read more like a rallying cry, a 'call to arms' to the readers.

'In view of the great national emergency all sections of our people must stand together. Not only those in the fighting line but those who are left to carry on the business of the nation, have a duty to perform.

There should be no scares, no line, no attempt to corner the necessaries of life, no private hoarding of supplies, no waste in any shape or form. Suffering there must unhappily be. Let everyone do his part to minimise it.

Let us remember also, that the paper money which the government is bringing into use is a great public convenience and just as good as gold, for it has the national credit behind it.

Employers of labour can and will do a great deal to help. Times of war affect newspapers very adversely, although popular opinion hardly realises it.

Notwithstanding this, the proprietors of the Essex County Chronicle series of newspapers will maintain their rate of wages in all departments, without any short time or reductions of staff.

Just as politicians have put aside their divisions, so we are sure that everyone who is able will lend a helping hand where he can. The people of the United Kingdom have a great ancestry, great position carries with it great responsibility, and this is the time when none is for party, but all are for the state.'

The following articles help give an overall flavour of how life was in those early days of the war, both on the home front and what had happened militarily in the first few days of the war. The first major development was the fighting which was taking place in and around the Belgian city of Liège where both sides sustained heavy casualties, which held back the German advance and allowed the Franco-British forces a short breathing space.

Requisitioning of farm horses

'Mr E.G. Prettyman MP raised a question in the House of Commons yesterday about the taking of farm horses now occupied in gathering in the harvests, for military purposes, and pointed out that purely on national grounds it was very important that these should not be interfered with. The Government and the War Office accepted this view, and orders have been given accordingly so that farm horses will not be taken except in extreme circumstances.'

During the war over one million horses were used in military service for a plethora of reasons, so it was clear to see their overall importance to the war effort, especially in the first few years before mechanically propelled vehicles became more readily available.

End of the farm strike

'The strike was formally ended on Tuesday night, and the men returned to work on Wednesday morning. The terms were a

compromise: the men to have 15s a week for farm labourers, 16s 6d cow-keepers, and 17s 6d for horse-keepers, with £8 for harvest. This is a 2s rise after a four month strike. The men gave up the original demand for £1 a week and a Saturday half holiday, and the farmers advanced the wages as shown. The compromise is the direct outcome of the appeal to patriotism over the strike by the Chief of the Essex Police.'

Presentation to Superintendent Laver

'Superintendent Laver of Grays, who is retiring from the Essex Constabulary after 37 years' service in different parts of the county, was on Friday, before the petty session commenced, presented with an illuminated address on vellum, an inscribed gold watch, and a purse of fifty guineas by the Justices of the Peace of the Orsett Division in the county of Essex, the members of the legal profession practising at the Grays Police Court, officials and corporate bodies in the district, and other inhabitants of the Orsett petty sessional Division, it being felt that some tangible acknowledgement should be made of the courteous and efficient manner in which he had carried out his duties as Superintendent under specially trying circumstances.

Sir T.B. Lennard, who presided, said it was the services he had rendered the bench that he had to thank Supt: Laver more particularly for and especially during the trying time of the strike. The Police altogether had a difficult time, and great praise was due to him for the modernisation and consideration they displayed and by which they were able to carry the matter through without more serious consequences.

Mr T.A. Capron, Magistrates Clerk, Mr H.J. Jefferies, Solicitor on behalf of the legal profession, and Inspector Page on behalf of the Police, added their quotas of praise and in response Supt: Laver said it was a great pleasure to receive the gift, but more especially to know he had done his work in such a way as to satisfy the public. With regards to the strike, it was due to the readiness of the men to do what he had asked them to do that they were successful.

Mr Capron added that he had received a bunch of letters of

a complimentary character with cheques for the subscriptions
and he had great pleasure in handing them to Supt: Laver.'

It would appear that Superintendent Laver was a very well respected and thought of individual to receive so many platitudes from so many different quarters.

To think that he began his service in 1876 is difficult to fully comprehend, but he was evidently very well thought of by everybody who had dealings with him, criminal types excluded of course; even his own men appeared to have been fond of him, which was no mean feat to achieve.

More Germans gathered in
The authorities have decided that known Germans on the London telephone exchange shall be disconnected.

Food prices under state control
Granulated sugar. 4d per lb
Lump sugar. 5d per lb
Butter. 1s 6d per lb
Cheese (Colonial). 9½d per lb
Lard (American). 8d per lb
Margarine. 10d per lb
Bacon (Continental). 1s 4d per lb
Bacon (British). 1s 6d per lb

It showed what state of affairs things were in when the government had to bring food prices under state control. A combination of factors came together to affect the prices of all food stuffs, causing the government to act before matters got out of control.

Food prices will always rise in a time of war especially when a nation is reliant in part on foreign imports as part of its basic day-to-day dietary needs. Add to this equation the shortages that occur because of panic buying and stockpiling of goods to increase the price. Racketeers and other greedy vendors added to the problem by increasing the price of goods they were selling.

Grays man's death at Purfleet
'At Tilbury on Thursday an adjourned inquest was held on George Crouch of 87 Grove Road, Grays, who met with injuries from which he died while engaged on the SS San Gregorio at Purfleet on the night of July 3. Deceased fell down the hatch into the hold. The jury returned a verdict of accidental death and added a rider that the ship was insufficiently lighted and that skeleton hatches should be provided.'

Health and safety was unheard of back in 1914. Accidents could and did happen on a regular basis without anybody facing criminal charges.

Drowned off Purfleet
'On Thursday an inquest was held on W M Allen 29, a greaser, of Upperton Road, New City Road, Plaistow, who was engaged at the steamship owners coal association wharf at Purfleet, and fell from the jib of the crane into the Thames and drowned. Verdict, accidental drowning.'

The following week's edition of the *Essex Newsman* carried on its theme of the patriotic approach to the war by encouraging young men to 'join up'.

Your King and Country need you
'Will you answer your country's call? Each day is fraught with the gravest possibilities, and at this very moment the Empire is on the brink of the greatest war in the history of the world.

In this crisis your country calls on all her young unmarried men to rally round and enlist in the ranks of her army.

If every patriotic young man answers her call, England and her Empire will emerge stronger and more united than ever.

If you are unmarried and between 18 and 30 years old, will you answer your country's call? And go to the nearest Recruiter – whose address you can get at any Post office and
JOIN THE ARMY TODAY
For full particulars apply at any of the following Depots.
COLCHESTER
CHELMSFORD

> *BRENTWOOD*
> *WESTHAM (The Cedars)*
> *STRATFORD (Artillery House)*
> *WALTHAMSTOW (Church Hill)*
> *All persons in the Chelmsford District wishing to join should apply at the Inquiry Office at the Headquarters of the Essex Territorial Force Association, Market Road, Chelmsford.'*

The locations where men could go to enlist increased over time, with both Southend and Grays being two such towns that were added to the list of locations where men could join up.

The main item of war news was still the fighting between German and British troops. There were lots of snippets of patriotic acts taking place on the home front all over the country, even though there wasn't too much news filtering through about the numbers of British military casualties.

A separation allowance had be set up for the wives and children of soldiers who were mobilized reservists, special reservists, members of the Territorial Force called up for active service and civilians enlisted for temporary service during war.

There was also a relief fund set up by the Prince of Wales to deal with distress caused by the war. It didn't, however, explain what the criteria were for receiving monies from the fund, who would administer it, how much would be awarded or how one applied to receive any funding from it.

The following article was also taken from the *Essex Newsman*, of 15 August 1914, a week into the war with Germany.

Tilbury Urban Council and the war

> *'On Wednesday a meeting of the Urban Council was held to consider what steps should be taken for local relief. Mr Brennan, the Chairman, said he expected there would be dislocation of shipping at Tilbury, and about 500 men would be thrown out of employment. He moved, "that with a view of providing employment, the Joint Sewerage Board be urged to proceed at once with the construction by direct labour of the proposed trunk sewer, or such portion thereof as may be deemed practicable". This was carried. It was also agreed to ask the local government*

board to sanction the council's housing scheme as speedily as possible, and if relief works and distress committees were formed.'

Many people had the real belief and expectation that the war would be over by Christmas; they were all proved to be right, but sadly it wouldn't be until Christmas 1918, that the war would finally be over and peace and goodwill restored.

This article was taken from the edition of the *Essex Newsman* dated Saturday 26 December 1914.

Local soldier awarded gallantry medal

'Private A. Milward of the 2nd Battalion, the Coldstream Guards and formerly a policeman at Tilbury Docks, was decorated on the battlefield with the Distinguished Conduct Medal, and promoted to the rank of sergeant.

As a policeman he was stationed at Tilbury for two years and removed to Epping this year.

The citation for his award of the Distinguished Conduct Medal read as follows:

"8574 Lance Serjeant A. Milward, 2nd Battalion Coldstream Guards – 17 December 1914. For gallant conduct. Has always volunteered and carried out successfully duties of an extraordinarily character, such as sniping and patrol work. Has shown great qualities of nerve and resource in difficult situations."'

Further enquiries showed that this related to Albert Milward. Having checked the British Army First World War medal roll index cards 1914-1920 for Albert Milward, he is shown as having being awarded the British War Medal and the British Victory Medal.

On the CWGC website, there is no record of either an A. Milward DCM or Albert Milward DCM which is a very strong indicator that he survived the war. We know he re-joined the army in 1914, or rather was recalled to the colours, after having previously served in the army before joining Essex County Constabulary.

Checking the 1911 Census for an A. Milward there is a match of a 19-year-old man (Albert) who coincidentally is shown as being a private in the 2nd Battalion of the Coldstream Guards, stationed at Ramillies barracks in Aldershot.

From the above article in the *Essex Newsman* dated Saturday 26 December 1914, we know that he joined the army in 1914 and that he had been a policeman for the previous two years. It would appear that he left the army soon after the 1911 Census was taken, joined Essex County Constabulary and at the outbreak of war was 'recalled to the colours'.

Eventually we managed to locate Albert's Essex County Constabulary record of service, which shows that he was born on 5 May 1891 in Hailsham. He was 5 feet 9 inches tall with a 38-inch chest, light brown hair, a fresh complexion and blue eyes.

It also shows that he was in the Coldstream Guards between 11 January 1910 and 10 January 1913. He was certified as being fit enough to become a police officer by the Essex County Constabulary on 11 January 1913 and sworn in on 7 February 1913. He was recalled to the colours at the outbreak of the war and re-joined the Coldstream Guards on 6 August 1914. He was with them for just over two years before leaving the army on 22 December 1916.

His record goes on to show that he was discharged from the army on 22 December 1916 as no longer being physically fit for war service. Despite this, he re-joined Essex County Constabulary the very next day. Just over six weeks later a report was submitted against him for misconduct; upon investigation it was found he was unfit for further service as a constable and he was permitted to resign on 8 February 1917.

Interestingly enough his Essex County Constabulary record of service doesn't show any misconduct matters against him or what ailment or illness it was that rendered him unfit for war time military service. It does show that he served at Tilbury Docks between 1 August 1913 and 10 February 1914. Today Tilbury Docks isn't the responsibility of Essex Police, it now has its own independent police force as part of the Port of London Authority Police.

Albert was transferred from Tilbury Docks to Epping police station where he served until 5 August 1914 when he was recalled to the colours. On re-joining Essex County Constabulary on 23 December 1916 he was posted to Harwich police station where he served for exactly one month, before being allowed to resign on 8 February 1917.

The following articles were taken from the *Chelmsford Chronicle* on Friday 29 June 1917.

'Private A.J. Burns, Essex Regiment who was reported missing and wounded on March 27, is now a prisoner in Turkey. His parents, who live in Kennington Cottages in Aveley, have received letters from him saying he is unwounded and in good health.'

With so many families receiving such sad news nearly every day throughout the war, how reassuring it must have been for Mr and Mrs Burns to discover that their son, albeit a prisoner of war in a foreign land, was safe and well.

'Mrs C. Wade, late of Chapel House, West Thurrock, now of Woodford Green, has learnt that her son, Lance Corporal A.E. Parmenter, of the Essex Regiment who was reported as being missing and wounded on April 12, is now discovered to be a prisoner of war and being held as such in Germany.'

The following articles were gleaned from the *Essex Newsman* from the edition of 2 September 1916.

'Lance Corporal A. Graygoose of Grays is reported as one of those killed. Essex Regiment.'

The CWGC website shows a Lance Corporal A. Greygoose (e instead of a), service number 12640 who was a member of the 2nd Battalion, the Essex Regiment when he was killed on 1 July 1916, the first day of the Battle of the Somme.

Albert Greygoose was born in Forest Gate, Essex and lived in Orsett. He is buried in the Sucrerie Military Cemetery, Colincamps in the Somme region of France. Locally he is commemorated on both the Orsett war memorial where his name is spelt Greygoose and also on the nearby Stifford war memorial, where his name is spelt Graygoose.

'Lance Corporal Arthur North of West Thurrock who was serving with the Essex Regiment, has been officially reported as having been killed. He was 23 years old.'

Arthur North was killed on 3 July 1916 in the early days of the Battle of the Somme. His body was never found and he is commemorated on the Thiepval War Memorial.

Other local casualties included: Lance Corporal Arthur Greaves, who was serving with the Australian Expeditionary Forces and was killed early in 'the great advance' towards victory on 26 July 1918. Arthur was the son of the late Arthur Greaves and Mrs Greaves of 9 Sydney Road, Tilbury Docks, Essex. He is buried in the Warloy-Baillon Communal Cemetery Extension on the Somme.

Private H. Hide of the City of London Regiment was killed in action on 20 July 1916. He was a Rifleman in the 2nd/17th Battalion of the London Regiment. Prior to joining the Army he worked at Tilbury Docks. He was about 30 years of age and left a widow and three children living at 20 Derby Road, Grays. Essex.

He is buried in Ecoivres Military Cemetery at Mont-St. Eloi in the Pas de Calais region of France.

The newspaper reported:

'The parents of Private E. Lloyd of the Royal Fusiliers, Mill Lane, West Thurrock, have received intimation that he was killed during the great advance in France. He is the second son whom they have lost, one having been killed at Mons early in the war. They have two other sons in the army.'

His full name was Ernest Lloyd and his family lived at 3 Mill Lane, West Thurrock, Essex. His brothers were David, James and Arthur Lloyd.

In the same edition of the *Essex Newsman* was the following humorous piece of news which must have been a welcome relief after all the bad news.

'At the Orsett Rural Council the medical officer of health, Dr Allington, reported that a Danish woman living in Tilbury, kept a large number of poultry under circumstances which were insanitary. She admitted to him that she kept an incubator in the house, while the neighbours declared that Turkeys and ducks could be seen roosting on the beds. The sanitary Inspector, Mr Hurst, agreed but added that the woman would not let him in

the house. "There's a dog there", he said. It was decided to make
an order that the nuisance must be abated.'

The local newspapers contained pages and pages of useful information,
not only about the sadness of families losing loved ones on the Western
Front and other theatres of war, but about other war-time matters which
showed, despite the country being engaged in fighting a bloody war
and losing hundreds of its young men every day, life still went on as
usual. They are a useful part of a historian's toolkit, providing a clear
and precise record of past events.

The following article appeared in the *Essex Newsman* on Saturday
2 September 1939.

> '*Mr Charles Spooner of 13 Maycroft Avenue, Little Thurrock, is on*
> *September 8 retiring from the service of the LMS Railway Company,*
> *in which he has been for fifty years, mostly as a signalman.*
>
> *For the last twenty years he has been in the signal box at*
> *Grays West. A native of Bulphan, Mr Spooner was living in*
> *Dagenham when he joined the old London, Tilbury and*
> *Southend Railway staff.*
>
> *He was at Rainham for a year as a porter before being given*
> *his first signal box. He is well known in the district as an*
> *exhibitor at flower shows, and has taken many prizes at the*
> *Orsett show. He has three sons and five daughters. Two sons*
> *gave their lives in the 1914-1918 war.'*

The two sons referred to in the article are Albert Charles Spooner and
Alfred Spooner. Albert Charles Spooner was a private in the East
Surrey Regiment when he was killed on 22 April 1915. He is
commemorated on Arras War Memorial in the Pas de Calais. Alfred
was a private in the 11th Battalion of the Essex Regiment and was 21
years of age when he was killed on 15 October 1916. He is
commemorated on the Thiepval Memorial on the Somme.

The names of both men are recorded on the Little Thurrock war
memorial as well as the one in Tilbury town centre.

Before enlisting in the Army both Albert and Alfred had followed
in their father's footsteps. Albert was a railway booking clerk and
Alfred a railway goods clerk.

CHAPTER 13

The Story of Joseph Farmer

Joseph Farmer was born on 17 March 1884 in the market town of Axminster in Devon. Like many of his peers, on leaving school he became a labourer before joining the army some time after April 1901. Job opportunities were very limited for working class people in the late eighteen hundreds. For men it tended to be either labouring or a few years in the army. Some were more fortunate and managed to obtain less arduous type work such as that of a shop assistant.

How or why Joseph turned up in Essex after leaving the army is not known. For a while he became a labourer before once again deciding to work in a disciplined environment. He became a police officer. He joined the Essex Constabulary on 7 December 1905 becoming Police Constable 256. His first posting was to Brentwood police station, he moved from there to Great Clacton, then on to Lambourne End, before being transferred to Tilbury police station in the early part of 1911.

In the 1891 census Joseph was only seven years of age and was living at 54 Wykes, in Axminster, where he lived with father Frank, two older sisters and a brother, an uncle and his elderly grandparents. His mother had died.

In 1901 Joseph was 17 years of age and was now living at 132 Higher Wyke in Axminster with his sister Mary Hooper, her husband Luke and their two young children. He was then shown as a farm labourer.

From the 1911 census taken on 2 April 1911, we know that he was living in Chadwell-St-Mary in Essex. He was a single man and living in single men's quarters in Dock Road, Tilbury along with two other police officers, William George Harrington, who at the age of 27, was the same age as Joseph, and Alfred William Jiggings who was 23. Of the three men, Joseph was shown as being the senior boarder.

Whilst serving there, Joseph met and married a local girl, Florence Ellen Pavitt, on 12 August 1912 at St John the Baptist Church at Tilbury Docks. They moved to 15 Railway Cottages in Tilbury. By the outbreak of war two years later they already had two young children and Florence was pregnant with their third child. Joseph had been transferred to Rochford Police station in Southend by now, but was still living with his family back in Tilbury.

Having previously served in the army with the Coldstream Guards, Joseph was, despite being a serving police officer, still an army reservist and was called up at the outbreak of the war. He became Private 4901 of the 1st Battalion of the Coldstream Guards.

Joseph's third child, a son, Joseph Charles Farmer, was born on 12 November 1914, but he would never get to see his father for Joseph Farmer died on 15 April 1917.

On arriving in France between 12 and 17 August 1914, the 1st Battalion of the Coldstream Guards had little involvement in the initial retreat from Mons as part of the British Expeditionary Force (BEF). However they became more involved as the months passed and the fighting became more severe.

Their first serious engagement took place on 14 September, the day after they had crossed the River Aisne. They eventually took up positions along the Chemin des Dames where they were met by a ferocious and sustained artillery bombardment which resulted in very heavy losses. In total they lost eleven officers and some 350 other ranks. At the end of the day Joseph Farmer, who had initially been recorded as missing, had in fact been taken prisoner by the Germans.

The following paragraph about that day is taken from the war diary of the Coldstream Guards.

'Lieutenant Colonel Ponsonby eventually collected the equivalent of about a company of his men and continued the advance, penetrating about a mile within the enemy's line and occupying a very forward position beyond the village of Cerny. Then followed some confused fighting in the fog that was very thick. For a time the Guards were able to hold their own, but in

the afternoon a heavy counter-attack, in which eighteen German battalions took part, was launched against the front held by the 1st Division. The Coldstream, Scots Guards and Cameron Highlanders made a gallant resistance and attacked in their turn, but the enemy's pressure was too great and they were eventually obliged to relinquish their positions.'

Some time later Joseph Farmer sent a postcard to his superior at Rochford police station, Superintendent Scott. It had been sent from a prisoner of war camp at Doeberitz in Germany. The card explained that Joseph had been taken prisoner by the Germans and was being treated as well as could be expected in the circumstances.

Joseph Farmer was transferred from the comparative safety of the PoW camp in Doeberitz to a region on the Eastern Front known as Mitau, in what is now Latvia. He died there on 15 April 1917.

The *Chelmsford Chronicle* reported on Friday 29 June 1917.

'Mrs J. Farmer of Railway Cottages, Tilbury, has been informed that her husband, Private Joseph Farmer, of the Coldstream Guards, who was taken prisoner after the Battle of Aisne in September 1914, died on 15 April 1917, aged 33 years. The deceased was for many years a Policeman stationed at Tilbury and latterly at Rochford. He leaves two young children.'

After his death a letter he had written whilst in captivity on the Eastern Front appeared in the Essex County Chronicle. It read as follows.

'I am with my old company, working in the trenches on the Russian firing line; we are under big gun fire all the time, and I was nearly blown to pieces today. We are told we are here because our government is treating German prisoners the same. Will you make this known to the public how we are treated and why, for it's awful here, but keep a good heart.'

Joseph Farmer was initially buried in Mitau but after the war his body and those of some of his colleagues were reburied in Nikolai cemetery in what today is Latvia. It would appear that Joseph died in hospital having been sent there suffering from a combination of exhaustion and starvation brought about through being over worked and under fed by his German captors.

On 5 September 1917, the Essex Police committee awarded Joseph's wife, Florence, the sum of £14.7.7d. What subsequently happened to her and her three children is not known.

CHAPTER 14

The Story of
James Edmund Stone

James Edward Stone was born in Poplar, London in 1894. He joined Essex Constabulary on 8 December 1914 aged 20 to become Police Constable 139. With the war ten months old he decided to enlist in the Army and did so at the recruiting office at Grays on 31 May 1915. He signed on as Gunner 101869 in the Royal Horse Artillery.

James initially saw action whilst serving at Gallipoli before moving with his Regiment to the Western Front in France in March 1916. At Beaumont Hamel, with 'B' Battery, 15 Brigade, Royal Horse Artillery, he took part in the Battle of the Somme until 6 July when he was seriously injured during the fighting. So bad were his wounds that although he was treated first at a casualty clearing station and later at a field hospital he subsequently died at a field hospital near Rouen on 2 August 1916. He is buried at the St Sever cemetery at Rouen.

On 16 December 1916, the then Chief Constable of Essex Constabulary, John Alfred Unett, informed his Police Authority of Gunner Stone's death. In December 1932, Unett gained the distinction of becoming the only Chief Constable in Essex to have died whilst still a serving police officer.

CHAPTER 15

West Tilbury Village Hall

West Tilbury lies in the extreme south of the county and is a quiet village community set in the beautiful Essex countryside. As well as being one of the district's seven conservation areas, it also sits on top of a ridge which looks out over the River Thames.

West Tilbury village hall has been set in its picturesque surroundings since 1924 when it was opened by Captain E.A. Loftus, in memory of the men of the village who had given their lives in the Great War. Inside there is an ornate plaque which records their names.

The hall was built using funds raised from donations made by local residents as well as the village's wealthier land owners, and continues to serve the community to this very day.

The names of those local men who fell during the First World War are recorded on a memorial tablet in St James's church and on a plaque at the village hall. There are nine names recorded on both of them.

'In loving memory of the men of this parish
who laid down their lives for their country
during the Great War 1914–1918.'

Herbert Plume BARNES (Royal Navy)
Stanley Cave CHIPPERFIELD (Royal Sussex Regiment)
James Henry DIPROSE (Essex Regiment)
Alexander Victor EMMERSON (Royal Field Artillery)
Henry George HONEY (Royal West Surrey Regiment)
Charles Frank HYDE (Middlesex Regiment)

Stewart Arch JACOBS (Royal Sussex Regiment)
Edward George PERKINS (HMS *Bostonian*)
William Ernest SPARROW (Mercantile Navy)

Herbert Plume Barnes was a Stoker 1st Class on board HMS *Hawke*, the sixth British warship to be given the name. She was a cruiser and was first launched on 11 March 1891 from Chatham Dockyard.

On 20 September 1911 she was involved in a collision with the White Star Liner, RMS *Olympic* in the Solent, the stretch of open sea which separates the Isle of Wight from the mainland. Thankfully this only resulted in damage to both ships with no loss of life.

The First World War was only two months old when HMS *Hawke*, commanded by Captain Hugh Williams, was struck by a torpedo fired from the German submarine, *U-9*. On 15 October 1914 HMS *Hawke* was sailing with her sister ship, HMS *Theseus* off the north-east coast of Scotland, when tragedy struck. The submarine's first torpedo missed HMS *Theseus*, which was the ship it was actually aiming at, and struck HMS *Hawke* igniting the ship's magazine and causing a massive explosion which ripped her in half. Captain Williams, twenty-six of his officers along with 497 of his men, all perished.

The seventy crew who survived the attack were fortunately picked up by the destroyer, HMS *Swift* and the steamer, HMS *Modesta*.

U-9 was launched on 18 April 1910. During the First World War she was responsible for the sinking of eighteen British ships.

On 22 September 1914 whilst patrolling the southern part of the North Sea, she sank three British armoured cruisers, HMS *Aboukir*, HMS *Hogue* and HMS *Cressy*, in under an hour and in doing so took the lives of 1,459 British sailors. She survived the war and surrendered on 28 November 1918 only to be broken up for salvage the following year.

Stoker 1st Class Herbert Plume Barnes was one of those who sadly perished on board HMS *Hawke*. His name, along with that of 18,663 lost souls, is recorded and remembered on the Naval Memorial at Chatham.

Stanley Cave Chipperfield was a private in the 7th Battalion of the Royal Sussex Regiment when he was killed on 21 May 1918. He was only 20 years of age. His parents, William and Emma Catherine

Acheux British Cemetery. (Commonwealth War Graves Commission)

Chipperfield, lived at 2 Bryanstone Road, West Tilbury, Essex at the time of his death. He is buried at the Acheux British Cemetery in the Somme region of France.

VIII Corps' collection station was placed at Acheux in readiness for the Battle of the Somme in 1916. Between April and August 1918 when Germany had what would turn out to be their last big offensive of the war, the Allied front line was within 8 kilometres of Acheux. There are 180 soldiers from the First World War buried there.

James Henry Diprose was a private in the 10th Battalion of the Essex Regiment when he was killed on 24 August 1918. He is buried in the Albert Communal Cemetery in the Somme region of France.

The town of Albert was held by French forces against the German advance on the Somme in September 1914. It passed into British hands in the summer of 1915 and was close to the front line during the fighting

Albert Communal Cemetery. (Commonwealth War Graves Commission)

in July 1916. It was captured by the Germans on 26 April 1918 and, before its recapture by the 8th East Surreys on 22 August in the Battle of Albert, 1918, it had been completely destroyed by artillery fire. There are 862 soldiers buried in the cemetery from the First World War.

The extension to the cemetery was used by fighting units and field ambulances from August 1915 to November 1916, and more particularly in and after September 1916, when field ambulances were concentrated at Albert. From November 1916, the 5th Casualty Clearing Station used it for two months.

Alexander Victor Emmerson was a driver with the 26th Battery, 17 Brigade of 43rd Royal Field Artillery when he was killed on active service in Flanders on 12 October 1917. He was the son of Laura Rathbone of 6 Bryanstone Road, West Tilbury, Essex.

Alexander enlisted early on in the war, on 16 August 1914. He was awarded the British War Medal, the 1914 Star and the British Victory Medal.

Dozinghem Military Cemetery. (Commonwealth War Graves Commission)

The first Battle of Passchendaele, during the final phase of the Third Battle of Ypres, began on 12 October 1917, the very day that Alexander was killed, in what was unusually wet weather for the time of year. It was an attempt by the Allies to gain ground around the area of Passchendaele. The heavy rain and energy-sapping mud, made movement difficult for the troops who were tired, cold, hungry and wet which was starting to affect morale. Because of the heavy mud it wasn't possible to get the heavy artillery pieces close to the front.

There were some 13,000 Allied casualties on that first day, over 2,500 of whom were soldiers from New Zealand, which still remains the worst military loss of life in one day in their history.

Alexander is one of 3,244 Commonwealth soldiers who are buried at the Dozinghem Military Cemetery in Poperinghe, West Flanders, in Belgium.

In July 1917, in readiness for the forthcoming offensive, groups of casualty clearing stations were placed at locations that had been nicknamed, Mendingham, Dozinghem and Bandaghem by the troops.

The 4th, 47th and 61st casualty clearing stations were posted to Dozingham and the military cemetery was used by them until early 1918.

William Ernest Sparrow was a trimmer in the Mercantile Marine, which was the forerunner to the Merchant Navy.

He was serving on board the SS *Orsova* on 14 March 1917 when she struck a German mine which had been laid by *UC-68*, just off the Eddystone Lighthouse and was forced to beach at Cawsand Bay. She was badly damaged and six of her crew, including William, were killed. Later she was towed to Devonport dockyards and repaired before being returned to her owners in 1919. She carried on sailing until she was eventually scrapped in October 1936.

She had begun life as a liner in 1909 for the Orient Steam Navigation Company, plying her trade between London and Australia and able to carry 1,310 passengers, before she was commandeered by the British Government as a troop carrier in 1915.

Henry George Honey was a private in the 7th Battalion of the Queen's (Royal West Surrey Regiment). His service number was 1410 and he was killed on 3 July 1916, on the third day of the Battle of the Somme aged 22 years. He was the son of George Herbert and Jane Honey who lived at 95 Orsett Road, Grays, Essex.

He is buried in the Corbie Communal Cemetery extension on the Somme.

Corbie Communal Cemetery. (Commonwealth War Graves Commission)

Corbie was about 20 kilometres behind the front when Commonwealth forces took the line from Berles-au-Bois southward to the Somme in July 1915. The town immediately became a medical centre, with No.5 and No.21 Casualty Clearing Stations based at La Neuville until October 1916 and April 1917 respectively. In November 1916 the front moved east but the German advance in the spring of 1918 came within 10 kilometres of the town and brought with it field ambulances of the 47th Division and the 12th Australian Field Ambulance.

The communal cemetery was used for burials until May 1918. The majority of the graves in the extension part of the cemetery are of officers and men who died of wounds in the 1916 Battle of the Somme. There are 1,167 burials from the First World War in both the main cemetery and the extension.

Charles Frank Hyde was born in Grays on 20 September 1896. He was one of nine children born to Frank and Harriet Hyde, who the 1911 Census shows as living at 8 Byranston Road, West Tilbury, Essex. Charles had four brothers, one, John who it is believed died at a very young age. Of the other three, Frank and Alfred were both old enough to have served during the war, but I can find no records showing either of them actually did, and youngest brother Frederick, would have only been fifteen years of age when the war finished. He also had four sisters, Alice, Annie, Florence and Doris. The 1901 Census showed the family as living a few miles away at 18 Wood Street, Grays.

Before the war, Charles was a ship's steward on passenger liners which sailed out of Tilbury Docks, that were situated close to where he lived at West Tilbury, which suggests he might have considered joining the Navy, but instead he chose the Army.

Charles enlisted on 8 March 1916 at the Warley Barracks, near Brentwood and became a private in the 1st/7th Battalion, Middlesex Regiment (Duke of Cambridge's Own), which was a Territorial Unit. He was later posted to the 3rd/7th and 4th/7th Battalions of the same regiment. He was killed on 10 April 1917. His Army service number was initially TF/202292, which was later changed to 6383. He has no known grave and his name is commemorated on the Arras Memorial.

Commonwealth forces moved into the Arras area during the Spring of 1916, taking over from their French counterparts. The Arras

Memorial commemorates the names of almost 35,000 Allied servicemen from Britain, New Zealand and South Africa, who died in the Arras region between the Spring of 1916 and 7 August 1918, and who have no known grave.

Stewart Arch Jacobs was born in 1891 in Balsham, Cambridgeshire. Both the 1901 and 1911 Census shows Stewart's father, Athur, as a publican, who ran the Three Horse Shoes Public House in Helions Bumpstead in Haverhill, Suffolk, where Arthur, his wife Eliza and their six other children lived.

Literacy was not widespread across the country at the beginning of the twentieth century. This is borne out by the three different spellings of his name. The Birth Index for England and Wales 1837 to 1915, records it as being Stuart. The 1891 Census shows it spelt as Stewart and the 1901 Census has it as Steward, all three of which refer to the same individual.

Stewart enlisted in the army and became a private in the 11th Battalion, The Royal Sussex Regiment and was killed on 3 April 1918, although the *Essex Newsman* dated 18 May 1918 shows a 'Pvt. S Jacobs of Helions Bumpstead' as missing. His service number was SD/5519. Stewart's name is commemorated on the the Pozières Memorial in the Somme region of France.

The memorial was unveiled on 4 August 1930 by Sir Horace Smith-Dorrien GCB GCMG DSO ADC, who was to sadly die only eight days later on 12 August. He had a distinguished military career dating back to the Battle of Isandlwana in South Africa during the Anglo-Zulu war. On 22 January 1879 a force of some 20,000 Zulus attacked a British column which consisted of 1,800 British, Colonial and Native troops along with 400 civilians. At the end of the day the 1,300 officers and men of the British led force had been killed. He also distinguished himself during the 2nd Boer War between 1899 – 1902. During the First World War he commanded the British II Corps at the Battle of Mons and the Battle of Le Cateau, where he fought a successful defensive action.

The Pozières Memorial contains the names of some 14,000 British and South African servicemen who were killed in the Somme region between 21 March and 7 August 1918 and who have no known graves.

Edward George Perkins was a fireman (Service number 609530) in the Mercantile Marine Reserve serving on board HMS *Bostonian*, an armed merchant ship, when it was sunk on 10 October 1917, having been commissioned only four months earlier on 16 June 1917.

It was torpedoed and sunk by German submarine *U-53* on 10 October 1917 when it was 34 miles off Start Point, Devon. Four members of the crew, including Edward, were killed.

CHAPTER 16

Lieutenant Colonel Sir Francis Henry Douglas Charlton Whitmore KCB CMG DSO TD JP, 1st Baronet

Sir Francis Whitmore was born in Leicestershire on 20 April 1872 and died aged 90 on 12 June 1962. He was buried with full military honours at Orsett parish church close to his home at Orsett Hall.

He had a long and industrious life and career, which for a large part had been spent in the military. His father, Thomas Whitmore, had also been a military man, serving as an officer in the Royal Horse Guards. He had inherited Orsett Hall as a gambling debt from its previous owner, Digby Wingfield.

Sir Francis Whitmore inherited it from his father when he died in 1907, by which time he had been an officer in the army for fifteen years. Initially he was commissioned into the 1st Essex Artillery Volunteers before transferring to the Essex Yeomanry.

He served in the second Boer War of 1899/1902 with the Imperial Yeomanry, which saw British forces eventually defeat fighters from the Transvaal and the Orange Free State. British losses were high due to both combat and disease. The latter half of the war had seen the Boers use guerrilla tactics extensively. The British reacted with a 'scorched earth' policy as well as one of internment against large swathes of the civilian populations of both the Transvaal and Orange Free State. This tactic proved to be somewhat of an 'own goal' for the British as it led to an erosion of support for the war back home in Britain.

During the First World War Sir Francis served as a cavalry officer and was promoted to the rank of lieutenant colonel in 1915 and ended up commanding the 10th Royal Hussars. He was awarded the Distinguished Service Order (DSO) in 1917 as well as being mentioned in despatches four times.

Whilst still a serving soldier he became a Justice of the Peace in 1898 and after the First World War he became the High Sheriff of Essex in 1922. He also served as the Lord Lieutenant of Essex from 1936 to 1958, having already been created Baronet of Orsett in 1954.

He was married twice. His first wife, Violet Houldsworth died in 1927 and his second wife, Ellis Johnson, with whom he had a son and a daughter, died in 2001. His baronetcy and estate were inherited by his son Sir John Whitmore, who sold Orsett Hall in 1968.

CHAPTER 17

PC George William Gutteridge

On 27 September 1927 PC489 George William Gutteridge, was shot dead in the early hours of the morning after stopping what turned out to be a stolen car.

Gutteridge left his home at 2 Towneley Cottages in Stapleford Abbotts, where his wife, son and daughter were sleeping, at just before 3am. He had moved to the Epping Division on 14 March 1922 and his assigned beat covered the villages of Stapleford, Lambourne End, Stanford Rivers and Kelvedon Hatch.

He made his way towards Howe Green to make a point with PC Sydney Taylor who covered the adjacent beat at Lambourne End. The two officers met at the top of Howe Green Hill where they chatted for about twenty minutes before PC Taylor left to go home to bed. Gutteridge stayed for a few minutes longer before doing the same.

PC George William Gutteridge. (With permission of www.murderpedia.org)

Gutteridge's dead body was subsequently found some 600 yards away from where he had met PC Taylor at the top of Howe Green Hill. Initially the circumstances of how Gutteridge met his death were not clear. At that time it wasn't even known if a vehicle had be involved or how many occupants would have been in it.

It later turned out that a vehicle had in fact been used in the murder. The car in question was a Morris Cowley which had been stolen the previous evening from London Road in Billericay, outside the home of the local doctor, Edmund Lovell.

Gutteridge had been shot four times in the face, the first two shots had been fired at close range as he approached the car, spinning him round so that he came to be propped up against the side of the road with his legs out in front of him. The third and fourth shots were fired directly into his eyes. There has been much conjecture over the years as to why this was done, but there

PC George William Gutteridge. (Wikipedia)

was a belief which prevailed amongst some at the time that when somebody died their eyes captured an image, almost like a photograph, of the last thing that they saw before dying.

As PC Gutteridge and his killers, Frederick Guy Browne and William Henry Kennedy are now all dead, we can only guess at the actual sequence of events that resulted in the officer's death. PC Gutteridge was still holding his pencil in his right hand when he was found some two and half hours later at just before six o'clock by William Ward, who at the time was delivering mail for the Post Office.

All four shots were fired from very close range and after PC Gutteridge's body was removed from the scene, two spent .45 bullets were discovered on the very spot where he had been lying.

Later that evening Dr Lovell's stolen car was found in Brixton, London with minor damage to the front mudguard. The vehicle was taken to nearby Brixton police station where it was searched by Detective Sergeant Hearn of the Metropolitan Police. Inside the car and under the front passenger seat, he found a shell casing and elsewhere in the car he discovered specks of blood.

At nearby Clapham Junction other Metropolitan Police officers were in Globe Garage waiting for a man by the name of Frederick Guy Browne, who was wanted for questioning in relation to the theft of

William Henry Kennedy &
Frederick Guy Browne.
(Photographs from
www.murderpedia.org)

another car. Their efforts paid off when Browne later drove into the garage. He was immediately searched and found to have in his possession pieces of medical equipment along with a number of live rounds of .45 ammunition. Then the car he arrived in was searched and a .45 Webley revolver was discovered on the inside of the driver's door. Further .45 rounds were discovered in the car along with another fully loaded .45 Webley.

When Browne's home in Battersea was searched yet another .45 Webley revolver along with more ammunition was discovered. The hunt was now on for Browne's 'associate', William Henry Kennedy, with whom he had committed previous crimes.

Murder Scene of PC Gutteridge. (Photograph with permission of www.
murderpedia.org)

When Kennedy was eventually arrested four months later on 25 January 1928 he tried to shoot the officer who arrested him, Sergeant Mattinson of Liverpool City Police, but fortunately for the officer, the bullet jammed in the barrel of the gun. Kennedy was brought back to London and interviewed.

The trial of Browne and Kennedy opened at the Old Bailey in London on 23 April 1928. Kennedy had made a statement claiming that it was Browne who had killed PC Gutteridge and that he had no prior knowledge of what he (Browne) was going to do, but he declined to take the stand and give evidence, so ensuring that he could not be cross examined. Browne on the other hand simply denied ever being at the scene of the murder or knowing anything about the crime.

Browne claimed to have been at home in bed with his wife at the time of the murder. Not surprisingly his claim was confirmed by his wife. It was also, however, substantiated by their landlady who made a statement to this effect, but neither Browne's wife or their landlady were called as witnesses at his subsequent trial.

Despite his claim to have been at home at the time of the killing, the gun which had been forensically proved to have killed PC Gutteridge, had been discovered in Browne's car.

Both men were found guilty of PC Gutteridge's murder after the jury had deliberated for only twenty minutes. They were both hanged, Browne at Pentonville Prison by Robert Baxter and Henry Pollard and Kennedy at Wandsworth Prison by Thomas Pierrepoint and Robert Wilson.

After having been found guilty and waiting for his sentence to be carried out, Browne is rumoured to have attempted to take his own life on more than one occasion. Ironically he tried to hang himself, cutting his own throat and going on a hunger strike which apparently resulted in him being force fed.

It would be interesting if the same trial took place today as it is still questionable that the balance of proof which determined their guilt was beyond all reasonable doubt.

The 1911 Census shows George William Gutteridge as living at Romford police station where he was lodging with three other young police officers along with the station's sergeant, Phillip Davis, his wife and their five children.

When he joined Essex Constabulary as Police Constable 489, on

Gray's Section House 1912. PC Gutteridge is on the back row. (Photograph with permission www.multipedia.org)

5 April 1910, he was initially stationed at Southend police station. From there he moved on to Romford police station, which at the time was part of the Essex policing area, and then on to Grays police station which is where he was when he enlisted in the British Army on 1 May 1918.

George William Gutteridge originally attested with a view to enlisting in the Army on 11 December 1915. He was on the Army Reserve for two and a half years, one would assume because as a serving police officer he was in a protected occupation. It is not clear whether he ultimately pushed his employers to be allowed to enlist or whether he was called up. In doing so he became Private 172937 and a member of the 2nd Reserve Battalion of the Machine Gun Corp, which was part of the 85th Training Reserve Battalion. Soon after he was transferred to the 4th Battalion of the Machine Gun Corps and sent to Clipstone Camp, in Grantham.

The description of Gutteridge taken down at his Army medical was that he was 5 feet 10¹/₂ inches tall, just under 11¹/₂ stones. He had short dark hair, a dark complexion, brown eyes with a 38³/₄ inch chest. He was born at Wimbotsham near Downham Market in Norfolk.

Whilst stationed at Grays police station he was living with his wife and daughter at 2 Southend Road, Little Thurrock, Grays, Essex.

Prior to joining Essex Constabulary on 5 April 1910, Gutteridge had already been in the army, but only briefly, when he served for five months with the 3rd Battalion of the Norfolk Regiment. He was demobbed from the Army on 23 February 1919 when he immediately re-joined Essex County Constabulary and went back to work at Grays police station.

There was a massive turnout for his funeral, not surprisingly in the circumstances, as it was a crime which had shocked a nation. His coffin arrived at Warley Cemetery in a magnificent horse-drawn carriage and was then taken to the graveside on the shoulders of six of his colleagues, who in turn were led by the Chief Constable, Captain Unett.

There is a roadside memorial at the spot where he was murdered.

The inscription on his gravestone, which was unveiled in 1928 by the then Chief Constable of the Essex Constabulary, Captain Unett, read as follows:

'In proud memory of George William Gutteridge, Police Constable, Essex Constabulary, who met his death in the performance of his duty on September 27th 1927.'

CHAPTER 18

The Wipers Times

The editor of *The Wipers Times* was Captain F.J. Roberts of the 12th Battalion of the Sherwood Foresters. In 1916 he was attached to the 24th Division which at the time was serving on the Western Front in France. He went on to reach the rank of lieutenant colonel before he retired from the army.

Captain F.J. Roberts. (Wikipedia)

The sub-editor of the magazine was Lieutenant J.H. Pearson. The two men intended to publish it on a weekly basis and right from the outset its satirical tone and gallows humour was obvious.

> *'But should our efforts come to an untimely end by any adverse criticism or attempts by our local rivals, Messrs Hun and Co, we shall consider it an unfriendly act and take steps accordingly.'*

The first edition was printed on 12 February 1916 with the last edition coming out in December 1918, but by then it had become *The Better Times*. During its existence it actually had six different names and there were only twenty-three editions in total. Twelve in 1916, seven in 1917 and the last four in 1918, the spread of which was in part a reflection of how the war had progressed over the years.

The Wipers Times came about because in early 1916 the 12th

Battalion of the Sherwood Forresters were stationed on the front line in Ypres, Belgium, which was pronounced by British soldiers as 'Wipers'. Whilst there they happened to find a printing press that had been abandoned by a local man. A sergeant from the 12th Battalion who had been a printer in Civvy Street before the war, salvaged it and printed off some sample pages; the newspaper was born and the rest, as they say, is history.

The paper was a mixture of satire and humour based on the life and experiences of soldiers in the trenches. Besides articles on the political situation of the day there were others about military regulations and overbearing senior officers, who appeared to have lost touch with any normal reality. The other topics included sex, alcohol, shelling and giant rats, as well as a never ending supply of poetry from both officers and other ranks.

Often produced in hazardous conditions, the paper acted as the voice of the common soldier. Not only did it reflect life as they knew it whilst they lived and fought in the trenches, but it also provided a window for later historians to have an insight into what life in the trenches was really like for these brave young men.

Life in the trenches could be quite traumatic for some, especially for those who had no option or choice about being there. One of the ways of dealing with the constant stresses which went hand in hand with the daily life of the trenches, was humour, which was in turn one of the main ingredients of *The Wipers Times*.

Captain Roberts and Lieutenant Pearson not only had a captive audience for their newspaper, but they could also empathise with the men who read it as they too had lived the same experiences, felt the same fears and yearned for the day when they too could return home to be warmly embraced by their loved ones.

Roberts and Pearson weren't stuffy out-of-touch officers who cared not a jot for their men, quite the opposite in fact, they wanted to help their comrades to deal with the fear and trepidation that went with life in the trenches. They knew that the best antidote for fear was that of laughter and humour, so that was what their magazines contained most of.

The reason why the publication continually changed its name was down to where the Division was located at any given time along the Western Front.

One of the more regular contributors was Gilbert Frankau an artillery man, but most of the contributors, who were undoubtedly officers, chose to keep their true identities hidden, through fear of retribution from those who were more senior in rank and who would have, more likely than not, viewed their connection to such a publication as not what would be expected of an officer and a gentleman.

Gilbert Frankau.
(Wikipedia)

Gilbert Frankau was an officer in the 9th Battalion East Surrey Regiment, having joined on 6 October 1914. He was born in London into a Jewish family. He was an educated man having attended Eton and then went into the family cigar making business.

He was invalided out of the army on 22 February 1918 because of injuries he had received during the war and later went on to become a writer of novels, calling on his own wartime experiences for some of his storylines, a few of which were turned into films.

CHAPTER 19

Inspector Richard Giggins – Tilbury Police

Richard Giggins was the police inspector at Tilbury police station in 1915, which was where he also lived with his wife Gertrude, Louisa Giggins and their son, Stanley Charles Giggins.

According to the 1911 Census, Richard and Gertrude had been married for twenty years and had three children, although Stanley was the only one living at home.

Richard Giggins had joined Essex County Constabulary in 1884 as a fresh-faced 19-year-old probationary constable. He had previously been a domestic gardener.

He was first stationed at Maldon. From there he was transferred to Southend where he remained until August 1887, before being moved on to Althorne where he remained for the next seven years. In April 1894 he was transferred to Steeple, then two years later he moved on to Purleigh where he remained until 2 October 1901.

Promotion and moves followed and by the 1911 census he was stationed and living at Harlow police station as an inspector. In May 1915 he was transferred to Tilbury police station by which time he had been a police officer for twenty-one years.

The year 1915 had another significance for Richard and Gertrude Giggins, it was the when their only son, Stanley, reached the age of 18. Whether his parents wanted him to or not isn't known, but as soon as he was old enough, Stanley enlisted in the army. He went off to nearby

Ilford and joined up, becoming a private in the 4th Battalion, the Essex Regiment. After completing his basic training at nearby Warley, on the outskirts of Brentwood, he travelled overseas and saw action at both Gallipoli and on the Western Front in France.

Stanley was one of the lucky ones; he survived the war, finally leaving the army on 13 July 1919, when he was officially demobilized at Purfleet Army Camp. This was one of the many locations, up and down the country, which soldiers who were either being de-mobbed or resigning from the army, had to attend before returning to their civilian lives.

Stanley's military record showed that his sobriety was 'satisfactory', which inferred that he drank quite a lot, but never enough to make himself too much of a nuisance to his superior officers. It also shows that he was both a rifleman and a stretcher-bearer during his service, both of which could be hazardous roles to carry out.

Whilst serving on the Western Front in France, he contracted diphtheria and was hospitalised for two months before being returned to his unit on 8 April 1917, having no doubt been glad of the respite from the fighting.

CHAPTER 20

Royal Magazine – Purfleet

What now houses the Purfleet Heritage and Military Centre in Centurion Way, Purfleet, on the north banks of the River Thames, was once a royal magazine for gunpowder.

When it was built in 1759, during the reign of King George II, it consisted of five large magazines for the storage of gunpowder for the king's army and navy, along with a proof house where the gunpowder was tested. The site was protected by two surrounding walls, consisting of an inner and outer section, along with a garrison of soldiers.

Each of the five magazines could house a maximum of 10,800 barrels, which was an exceptionally large quantity of gunpowder to keep in one location.

It was built during the Seven Years' War which took place from 1754 to 1763. This meant the gunpowder stored at the Purfleet magazine would have been in almost constant demand. It was a world war involving most of the great powers of the day and affected Europe, North America, Central America, the west coast of Africa, India and the Philippines.

The war was driven by the antagonism that existed between Great Britain and Germany on the one side and the Bourbon dynasty of France and Spain, on the other. Their dislike of each other came about largely because of their overlapping interests in the areas of colonialism as well as their trading routes.

By 1763 most of the warring factions had signed peace treaties with each other which effectively brought the war, during which an estimated one million people were killed, to an end.

The magazines remained in use until 1962 when the Ministry of Defence (MOD) sold them and the land on which they stood, to Thurrock council.

In the late 1960s, four of the five magazines were demolished to make way for housing whilst the fifth was kept for use as a council storage facility before becoming a museum and heritage centre in 1994.

Behind the old Purfleet clock tower garrison entrance is now a housing estate which, not surprisingly, is known locally as the Garrison estate.

A large British army camp went up in Purfleet during the early stages of the First World War which consisted of a combination of wooden huts and tents. Another camp went up at nearby Belhus Mansion, both of which were in place by April 1915 and at their peak accommodated some 10,000 troops at a time.

Whilst looking for information concerning Purfleet we came upon the following entry from July 2008 on a 'forum' style website (www.directplaces.co.uk).

It relates to a discussion in the Houses of Parliament on 21 November 1911, Hansard HC Deb 21 November 1911, and volume 31 c1009.

'*Mr Hamersley asked the Under Secretary of State of War, Colonel Seely the following question: "How many rifle ranges have been obtained, and made available for the use of the Regular and Territorial Forces since the 27th March, 1911, in addition to those that were in use at that date; has any land been purchased or acquired since the 27th March 191, for rifle ranges; if so, in what localities and at what price; have any rifle ranges that were in use on the 27th March 1911, been closed since that date; and, if so, in what localities and for what reason?"*

The Under Secretary of State for War (Colonel Seely): "With regard to the first part of the question, fifteen additional open classification ranges will be available for use next musketry season, five of which are old ranges re-opened and adapted for modern conditions. With regard to the remainder of the question, land has been purchased at Newton (Isle of Wight), Holcombe and Purfleet, for about £20,000 in all. Firing rights have been acquired on annual agreements in various localities for the purpose of extending danger areas of existing ranges, and land has been acquired on annual tenancies for thirty yard ranges."'

Even back in 1911 the threat of war appears to have been an ever present one, which was bubbling away just underneath the surface.

The Purfleet Musketry Camp first opened in 1914 at the outbreak of the war and was used by both Regular and Territorial Units of the British Army.

During the Second World War it was a Machine-Gun Training School for the London district as well as a D-Day marshalling area for British troops before they took part in the Normandy landings. It occupied a site west of Tank Hill Road, near to where the powder magazines were located and adjoining the rifle ranges on Aveley marshes.

From the 18th Division History:

'In September 1914 a train arrived at Purfleet Railway station, known as Purfleet rifle ranges, bearing 1000 volunteers of Kitchener's New Army, 300 of them were from Norfolk and had enlisted in the East Surreys.

There were not enough blankets to go round; the food was coarse; there were no recreation huts, no dining huts; no canteens such as the regular recruits found in barrack life, but the men's mood was to make the best of things.

Recruits were billeted in tents on the rifle range, which was no more than marshland alongside the River Thames. Their conditions worsened as winter approached and they were moved to higher ground at nearby Aveley until huts were erected on the range site.'

The ranges were still being used well into the twentieth century by the Territorial Army and in more recent times by specialist firearms units of the Metropolitan Police, as recently as 1981.

CHAPTER 21

Orsett & Grays Volunteer Aid Detachment Red Cross Nurses

Volunteer Aid Detachment nurses or VADs, the acronym with which they became known, really became established during the First World War through a combination of the War Office and the British Red Cross.

They had originally been formed in August 1909 to provide both nursing and medical assistance during a time of war, because of a fear that there would be a shortage of nurses should hostilities break out.

The VADs were trained by the British Red Cross Society in such roles and skills as first aid, making beds, how to give a patient a bed bath, and cleanliness.

It can be seen that even four years before the war had actually begun, there were well-founded fears that a war was going to happen and that it was simply a case of when rather than if.

After the outbreak of the war in August 1914, the Order of St John and the British Red Cross joined forces to form the Joint War Committee. Their purpose was to raise money and pool their collective resources under the banner of the Red Cross, which was universally recognised for the good work which it already carried out.

The Joint War Committee was the first to supply motorised ambulances to the battlefields in France and Belgium. This proved to be much more effective than their previous horse drawn counterparts. The first motorised ambulances financed by the Joint War Committee arrived in France in September 1914. These weren't sent by the British Government, but as a result of monies raised by voluntary public donations.

VADs predominantly worked within the UK but once the war began all that changed and where ever there was a theatre of war there were VADs not too far behind. They were so appreciated by the soldiers who they tended and cared for, that they were also affectionately known as Very Adorable Darlings.

The VAD's first national commandant was Katherine Furse.

The following is taken from the Essex Publication, *The British Red Cross Society, the County Branches: their organisation and work during the first months of the war.'* (Volume one edited by A.K. Lloyd.):

> *'Two members of this Detachment have served abroad. Miss Florence Brooks, who went to Serbia and did Red Cross work for six months, and Miss Gladys Brooks, who also went to Serbia for the same period of time. Four members are doing Red Cross work at Gravesend Red Cross Hospital, and have been engaged there for many months. Working parties have been held, and consignments of medical supplies have been sent to Dunkirk, Antwerp, and Serbia, these supplies having been purchased with funds collected by the Detachment.'*

At the start of the war there were 40,000 VADs; by the end of it in 1918 that number had more than trebled to 126,000. Their bravery, in what were quite often extreme conditions, was beyond question. In total 243 of their number were killed, 364 were decorated with gallantry awards and another 1,005 were Mentioned in Despatches. That so many were recognised for their bravery is a remarkable achievement.

The Commandant of the Orsett and Grays section, or Essex 12, to give it its official title, was Mrs Whitmore, of Orsett Hall, wife of the distinguished Lieutenant Colonel and later Sir Francis Henry Douglas Charlton Whitmore.

In 1914 the executive committee of the Essex Branch of the Red Cross consisted of the president, the Countess of Warwick, the director,

Lieutenant Colonel J. Colvin and the secretary, Colonel G.H. Coleman.

Soon after Britain's entry in to the First World War in August 1914, the number of Essex Red Cross staff totalled some 1,800.

There were a total of thirty-three Auxiliary hospitals which were covered by the Essex Branch of the Red Cross. These were designated as either class 'A' or class 'B' category hospitals; twenty-three were in class 'A', with the remaining ten being class 'B'.

Class 'A' hospitals were typically better equipped and had higher standards of care. This wasn't an issue of officers and other ranks receiving different treatment, the care was of a higher standard at the class 'A' hospitals, simply because it had to be because of the health of the men they were dealing with, regardless of rank. Patients were received directly from military hospitals or transport ships returning to Britain from the different theatres of war.

The hospitals in the class 'B' category generally only received patients who had initially had their wounds tended to in the class 'A' hospitals. Once they had been removed from the 'at risk' list and were deemed well enough to recuperate, they were then transferred to the class 'B' hospitals.

Many different buildings were considered suitable to accommodate hospitals, including Union Workhouses and hotels, such as the Overcliff Hotel at nearby Westcliff-on-Sea, which was situated right on the sea front.

Unfortunately, both the membership and branch records of the Orsett and Grays section (Essex 12), as well as the work which they performed, have not survived. All that the Red Cross records currently show are the details of three of the section's members: Commandant Violet Frances Elizabeth Whitmore OBE, Florence Brooks and Gladys Muriel Brooks MBE.

By 1915, there were 2,778 voluntary members undertaking a range of British Red Cross tasks in the Essex area. Male detachments in the area were limited due to many joining the Royal Army Medical Corps or other units on the continent. Lectures were regularly held in First Aid, Hygiene and Sanitation in order to train potential VADs.

Certificated volunteers were able to professionally care for the sick and wounded patients arriving home from the war. Alhough the majority of VADs worked in Essex and surrounding counties, a number of them were posted abroad.

Around thirty members of various women's detachments served abroad in countries such as Egypt, France and Serbia. Examples of this were Miss Nonie Craig and Miss Dorothy Poole who went abroad and worked in Mentone, France. A number of detachments were not mobilised throughout the course of war, yet contributed to the war effort, by helping in working parties and with the provision of medical supplies.

Men's detachments were responsible for the transportation of wounded soldiers who arrived at the county's train stations or ports, such as those at Tilbury Docks. From there the wounded would be taken to one of the local designated military or auxiliary hospitals, which received soldiers at any hour of the day or night. As well as acting as ambulance drivers, male detachments also acted as night orderlies at the hospitals.

A number of additional voluntary initiatives were established during the First World War. Provisions were made for 'rest stops' at train stations in order to feed hungry soldiers waiting to be transported to local hospitals or who were continuing on to other locations by train. There were around forty to fifty working parties scattered amongst the Essex branch, who were enthusiastically making garments and other similar articles for use in some of the hospitals.

Fundraising ideas took many forms, all of which were aimed at raising funds for the support of soldiers both home and abroad. The 'Our Day' campaign in 1915 raised a total of £5,123.5s.8d. Additionally, donations in the same year raised £4,479.18s.1d. towards the funding of Auxiliary hospitals in the Essex area. It has to be remembered that these were staggering amounts of money for the day. Another £900 was raised for the purchase and upkeep of two ambulances that were to be used in France and Belgium.

Florence Brooks lived at 'Duvals' in Grays, Essex and was aged 34 in 1911. The VAD membership card for Gladys Muriel Brooks MBE, shows that she lived at Stifford Lodge, near Grays. It also shows that although she was a member of the Essex 12, which was the Orsett & Grays VAD section, she actually worked at the Rosherville and Ingress Abbey Hospital in Gravesend, Kent.

The British Red Cross membership and service card for Florence Brooks, clearly shows that, like Gladys, Florence also served in Serbia prior to the start of the First World War. For any section to have had one experienced member would have been extremely beneficial, but to have been in the fortunate position of having had two, would have been a real bonus.

Their collective experience would have been invaluable, not only in the duties which they were individually able to undertake, but in the help and assistance that they would have been able to pass on to other colleagues with whom they worked. These were both difficult as well as unprecedented times in an age when the role of women was still seen in the main as that of mother and home maker. The Suffragette movement was still only in its infancy in the early years of the twentieth century, which puts into context just how much the VADs actually achieved when measured against the social stigmas and expectations of the day.

One of the other membership cards which survives from those years is that of Violet Frances Elizabeth Whitmore OBE. It shows that she was a member of the British Red Cross throughout the First World War and that between 18 May 1917 and 28 November 1918, she was working at the Orsett Auxiliary Military Hospital. Despite this commitment, she was also the commandant of the Grays Division of the British Red Cross.

CHAPTER 22

HMS *Clan McNaughton*

HMS *Clan McNaughton* was originally launched on 28 June 1911 as a passenger cargo ferry owned by Clan Line Steamers Ltd of Glasgow, but was converted to an armed merchant cruiser. She was captained by Commander Robert Jeffreys of the Royal Navy Reserve, when she foundered during a storm in the unforgiving seas of the North Atlantic on 3 February 1915. The ship went down and all those on board, which included 20 officers, 220 ratings, as well as 37 members of the Royal Marines Light Infantry were lost. It was the biggest single loss of life that Thurrock as a community suffered in a single day from a single incident during the entire First World War.

There were thirty-five men from the Thurrock area serving on the ship when it went down, all of whom are commemorated on the Grays War Memorial. Such a huge loss to one community would have been absolutely devastating. A tragedy that was certainly unparalleled for Thurrock as far as the First World War was concerned. It must have been on par with the towns and villages that provided the 'Pals' Battalions for Kitchener's Army and the massive losses their communities suffered when their men folk were killed in their droves.

The ship had been requisitioned by the War Department for the Royal Navy on 14 November 1914 and subsequently fitted with guns at Tilbury docks. It is an interesting point to consider, for a vessel that was designed and intended to be used as a passenger ferry and not for military purposes, how having heavy guns fitted to her might perhaps have affected her balance and buoyancy, especially in such extreme weather conditions as the *Clan McNaughton* experienced on 2 February 1915.

Before the war, she had sailed out of the same port on her way to India, which was the route she plied her trade on as a merchant cargo ship.

On Thursday 25 February 1915 the following article appeared in the *Sunderland Daily Echo and Shipping Gazette* newspaper about the disappearance of HMS *Clan McNaughton*.

Sea War
Armed Merchantman Lost
With 280 Officers and Men
Missing for three weeks

The following was issued last night by the Press Bureau:

The Secretary of the Admiralty regrets to announce that HMS Clan McNaughton, *an armed Merchant Cruiser (Commander Robert Jeffreys, RN) has been missing since 3rd February, and it is feared that the vessel has been lost. Unsucessful search was made and wreckage, supposed to be of this ship has since been discovered.*

The last signal from the Clan McNaughton *was made in the early morning of February 3rd, and it is feared that she was lost during the bitter weather which prevailed at the time.*

About forty members of the crew belonged to Tilbury and 30 to Gravesend and district.

The Admiralty last night issued a list of 20 officers and 260 men who were on the vessel when last heard of.'

It is a matter of debate whether the reason for the three week delay by the Admiralty in making the announcement of the loss of the *Clan McNaughton* was down to war time secrecy or nothing more sinister than allowing a period of time to search for the vessel and crew before informing the public of the loss.

The list of those men from the Thurrock area who died as a result of the loss of the ship is as follows:

Allen G.G. was a steward from Grays
Ambrose E.G. was a fireman from Grays
Batt A. was an assistant cook from Tilbury
Benson F.J. was a 2nd steward/storekeeper from Grays
Bikford F. was a 2nd cook from Tilbury
Biggs P.C. was a writer from Grays
Boyle H. was a trimmer from Grays
Bushell A. was a fireman from Little Thurrock
Chapple R. was a greaser from Grays
Chatting W. was a fireman from Grays
Cheeseman W. was a trimmer from Grays
Clarke A.H. was a trimmer from Grays
Curtis W.J. was a steward from Grays
Davis A. was a ship's steward from Grays
Dawson W. was a steward from Grays
Dennis F. was a trimmer from Grays
Dodge S. was a baker from Little Thurrock
Dunn R. was a painter from Little Thurrock
Finch J. was an assistant donkey man from Tilbury
Frost E. was a leading fireman from West Thurrock
Gentry G. was a fireman from West Thurrock
Hardwicke C. was a trimmer from Tilbury
Hunter A. was a greaser from Tilbury
Jackson P. was a fireman from Grays
Jones A. was a fireman from Grays
Long F. was a trimmer from Grays
Macey V. was a fireman from Tilbury
Palmer A. was a steward from Tilbury
Pryer A.T. was a leading stoker from Grays
Redshaw H. was a fireman from Grays
Richards T. was a fireman from Grays
Rouse W. was a trimmer from Grays
Smith J.W. was a donkey man from Tilbury
Stillaway W. was a fireman/store keeper from Grays
Toulson C. was a 2nd cook from Grays
Tredwell W. was a fireman from Tilbury
Williams J. was a greaser from Grays

The names of all of the Thurrock men who lost their lives with the sinking of HMS *Clan McNaughton* are commemorated locally on the war memorials in Tilbury and Grays, as well as on the Naval Memorial at Plymouth.

An interesting aside to this story is that of Carpenter's Mate Leonard Banks from Grays. The *Portsmouth Evening News* of 1 March 1915 included a report about Leonard. He was 31 years of age and a member of the crew of HMS *Clan McNaughton* but had been sent home just before the ship set sail on what would be her last voyage, suffering from gastritis. He was at home with his wife, Alice, and their 5-year-old son, Sydney, at 39 Oak Road, Grays, recuperating and awaiting further orders. Whilst at home a telegram arrived for his wife from the Admiralty advising her that the *Clan McNaughton* had been lost at sea along with her husband and all the rest of the crew. Leonard's name had appeared in all of the newspapers that reported the loss of the ship, listing him as one of the missing crew

One can only imagine the look of confusion on her face when she opened the telegram. For Leonard, fate had taken a hand in his destiny and had decided it wasn't his time to die. He survived the war.

CHAPTER 23

Kynochs Munitions Factory

The Kynochs Munitions Factory was located on land near to Shell Haven Creek and Fobbing. The area had originally been the 750-acre Borleys Farm. The founder of Kynochs was George Kynoch who was born at Peterhead, Aberdeenshire in 1834. Although he fell out with the board and resigned in 1888, dying in 1891 whilst living in self-imposed exile in South Africa, the company has kept the name to this day.

Building work on the Kynochs munitions factory had begun in 1895 and it opened for business two years later and, although already quite a sizeable operation, its capacity was improved accordingly with the ever increasing demands for all kinds of munitions because of the First World War. The site also included a housing estate for its workers, which became known as Kynochtown.

In the early years of the twentieth century the company began to struggle, but within weeks of the outbreak of war the company obtained contracts to make an additional 3 million cartridges a week, which soon increased to 7.5 million. Other contracts followed for shell cases, detonators, cordite, acetone and the like.

With the outbreak of war Kynochs factories at Witton in Birmingham, where they made percussion caps and Shell Haven and Fobbing, where they made cordite, guncotton, gunpowder and cartridges, both had to expand to cope with the extra demand. This meant that hundreds of women were employed on very long shifts, being paid 4d an hour. Many of these women came from the nearby Pitsea and Vange areas. The factories were obviously vulnerable to air attacks. The wardens at

Southend-on-Sea or Shoebury would send special telephone messages of an anticipated attack and the workers would shelter where they could or just watch the action. Being an essential part of the war effort, Kynochs, and no doubt the Pitsea explosives factory, were guarded by soldiers.

Men also worked at the factory. Some of them were even given an exemption from being called up into the army as working at the factory was classed as essential war work.

To support the new factory a new town was born, with houses, a shop and a club. There was a school, a cricket and a football team and a new hotel on Canvey, just across the stream. With the start of the war, a hospital came along with fire and police station, all to great acclaim.

The factory was open around the clock, twenty-four hours a day with workers having to work either twelve-hour days or twelve-hour nights. It was an extremely dangerous place to work, not only because of the unhealthy and potentially volatile substances which were made there, but because of the constant threat of manufacturing-related explosions as well as bombing raids from the German Zeppelins, who were attacking London and Eastern coastal areas which included south-east Essex.

Kynochs also built a railway line, known as the Corringham Light Railway, which had a passenger line from the factory to Corringham as well as a goods branch from the factory to Thames Haven, which allowed ships to dock close by, making it much easier for components to be delivered to the factory and the finished goods to be sent out.

In 1919 with the demand for their products having greatly reduced, the Kynochs factory closed. The name Kynochs became part of Nobel Industries which in turn became Imperial Chemical Industries. The Kynochs site and the Corringham Light Railway were taken over by coal merchants, Cory Brothers Limited of Cardiff, with a view to building an oil storage depot, and Kynochtown was renamed Coryton.

Besides providing an overview of the factory, what it did and how it came into existence, it is always good to try and show the human side of some of those who were part of it.

Percy Robert Chittock who lived in Vange prior to the war and who was later to join the Royal Horse Artillery, worked at Kynochs as a charge hand. He travelled to the site on the Corringham Light Railway. It was on his travels back and forth to work that he met his future wife

Langdon Hills Women's Institute. (Stephen Wynn)

Clara, who also worked at Kynochs. She had to dress in an all-white uniform and white boots so that the sparks did not catch her skin.

Percy and Clara married at Holy Cross Church in 1920 after Percy had returned safely from the war. Clara was born in Bow in 1892 and went to Atley Road School which was renamed the George Lansbury Primary School in 1951. George Lansbury was the person who supported Joseph Fels, the originator of the Dunton Farm Colony in Laindon.

At Kynochs various types of entertainment were organised and although sport, especially men's sport was restricted because of the lack of male personnel, Kynochs had a ladies' football team that played in a local female league.

Soon after Kynochs closed in January 1919 a sale took place which continued for four days. Items for sale included portable buildings, plant, machinery, tramlines etc. Some of the huts from the women's colony which had been erected so that they did not have to go home late every night, were purchased by locals and re-erected elsewhere as private dwellings. One such building was purchased by Frederick Jobson for £100 and was re-erected in Samuel Road, Langdon Hills by volunteer labour. It has been known as 'The Hut' ever since. Initially it had two billiard tables, a table tennis table and a stage erected to provide a centre for music, drama and general entertainment, showing just how big the hut actually is. The building still stands to this day and is now the home of the Langdon Hills Women's Institute.

CHAPTER 24

From Around the District

Prisoner of War Camps in Thurrock

There were German prisoner of war camps at Horndon House Farm, which held forty men, Puddledock Farm and Wouldhams Quarry in West Thurrock. The latter housed 150 German prisoners and Puddledock Farm had its moment of history when a German PoW escaped from there in July 1918. His name was Paul Simonitias and he was aged 22.

His experience of freedom was only short lived as he was re-captured the next day at nearby Warley, although what he was doing there isn't clear by any means. It can only be assumed that he had taken a wrong turning somewhere along the way and not realised where Tilbury was in relation to where he was being held as a prisoner.

It is not recorded what his punishment for escaping was, perhaps a loss of certain privileges for a period of time.

Although there were lots of PoW camps scattered throughout Great Britain at the time, the recording of their exact location, the names of those who were held there and what they were required to do, has unfortunately been poorly recorded in most cases, if at all.

More information appears to be available locally, held by museums or historians but even this is sporadic. If official records were initially retained by local authorities or the government of the day, they have either been lost or destroyed over the years as very little information about them survives to this day.

One wonders if the main reason for the lack of any official records having survived is because of a desire by the authorities not to panic the public by highlighting how many Germans were actually detained in camps up and down the country.

Orsett Workhouse Infirmary
Like most towns in the early 1900s, Orsett had its own workhouse which catered for the less fortunate from the surrounding parishes. Records show that there had been a workhouse in Orsett as far back as 1725, although the one which existed in the early 1900s wasn't built until 1837.

In those times there was no such thing as the welfare state or an old age pension. Those whose working days were over and who didn't have children to look after them, might end up in the workhouse to see out the rest of their days.

For each year the war dragged on the need for more and more hospital beds at home for returning wounded soldiers, increased massively. In 1917 the Orsett Workhouse Infirmary (or the Orsett House Isolation Hospital as it was also known), provided part of its facility to be used as a military hospital to help with an ever-increasing need. In the same year it was decided that only people who were ill would be admitted to the workhouse. Its use as a military hospital facility ceased in March 1919. There was also a dedicated military hospital at nearby Purfleet.

Orsett Basket Works
Orsett also had a basket works which was the brain child of Lieutenant Colonel Sir Francis Whitmore of Orsett Hall. It was funded by the Ministry of Labour and was established for soldiers who had been injured and disabled whilst fighting for king and country. Sir Francis Whitmore had served in the First World War and most of the men who worked at the basket works, had served in his regiment.

The idea was to provide these ex-soldiers with skills which they could use to help find other suitable civilian employment. The works were located at Pound Lane in Orsett.

There was even a nearby plantation established where the willows that were used for making the baskets, were grown. All different kinds of baskets were made there, including picnic hampers.

It eventually closed on 10 March 1939, just before the outbreak of the Second World War, not for financial reasons or the onset of an impending war, but because sadly, all of the original workers had retired and there were now insufficient men interested enough in wanting to learn and carry on the skills of basket making.

What had started out of a need to provide, not baskets, but jobs, skills and a worthwhile purpose for young men who had been wounded, had sadly and abruptly come to an end just at a time when ironically it could have once again served a very useful purpose.

South Ockendon Farm Colony
At the outbreak of war the South Ockendon Farm Colony was owned by the West Ham Distress Committee. During the war it was taken over by the Army and became a large tented military camp and by the end of the war it had become a German PoW camp.

The Defence of the Realm Act, or DORA as it was often referred to, was brought in at the beginning of the First World War. The Act provided numerous sweeping and often controversial emergency powers for the government to use in a time of war. One of these powers allowed the army to commandeer land for military use as it saw fit.

In 1905 Little Mollands, once part of the South Ockendon Hall estate, was bought by West Ham County Borough Council for use as a farm colony to provide three months' relief work for men who were not entitled to be paid unemployment benefit. The men who worked at the colony would each receive ten shillings per week, which is only 50p in today's money. The cost of accommodating and feeding them was estimated to be thirty shillings, or £1.50 for each man per week.

CHAPTER 25

The 1918 'Flu Epidemic

The influenza pandemic that spread across the world between 1918 and 1919 is estimated to have claimed the lives of between 50 to 100 million people.

Battery Sergeant Major R. Currie who was stationed at Coalhouse Fort, died of 'flu on 27 November 1918, followed six days later by his wife Daisy Alice Currie who passed away on 2 December 1918, yet another victim of the 'flu. They were buried in the nearby churchyard at St Catherine's Church which is situated immediately outside of Coalhouse Fort. Sergeant Major Currie's grave is today marked with a Commonwealth War Graves Commission headstone; what makes it somewhat unusual is the fact that the name of his wife, Daisy Ann, is also inscribed on it.

Headstone of Battery Sergeant Major Currie. (Stephen Wynn)

The war had touched most people throughout the country, either directly or indirectly. There weren't many families who had a son that went off to fight in the war, who didn't experience the pain of either losing a loved one or having one return damaged physically or mentally. For these same communities to then have to deal with further losses due to the 'flu pandemic, must surely have made many question their faith and Christian beliefs.

It is estimated that some 150 Thurrock residents died of influenza.

The 'Spanish 'Flu', as the pandemic was named, was an unusually severe and deadly strain of avian influenza which was extremely infectious. It is thought have been one of the most deadly pandemics in the history of mankind.

The virus caused an unusual number of deaths, mainly because this particular virus infected lung cells, leading to over stimulation of the immune system. This, coupled with the fact that medical treatments were nowhere near as advanced as they are today, resulted in a high proportion of fatalities.

In contrast to other recorded pandemics, which mostly attack and kill the old and the very young, the 1918 pandemic killed unusually high numbers of young adults.

The term 'Spanish Flu' came about simply because Spain was the only European country where the press were printing unrestricted reports of the outbreak, which had already killed thousands of men in the armies fighting in the First World War. Other countries, including Britain, suppressed the news from the masses in order to reduce the chances of unrest and to guard against panic and to keep public morale high.

CHAPTER 26

The War Memorials

In the following chapters we look at the war memorials that can be found in the towns and villages that make up today's Thurrock district. There are thirteen in total, if you include the large wall plaques which are situated at the Port of London Authority (PLA), London Cruise Centre terminal at Tilbury Docks. The memorials in question are at: Aveley, Bulphan, Chadwell-St-Mary, Grays, Horndon-on-the-Hill, Little Thurrock, Orsett, Purfleet, South Ockendon, Stanford-Le-Hope, Stifford, Tilbury (Clock Tower) and Tilbury Docks (Port of London Authority).

Most were erected in the early 1920s to commemorate the men from the individual towns and villages who had paid the ultimate price having answered the call to serve king and country.

Such events were nothing to do with any government backed initiatives or an official desire to raise civilian morale after four years of war. Those responsible for the building of all of these memorials were people from within the community. They were local dignitaries, wealthy individuals, friends and relatives of those who had gone off to fight and who sadly, had never returned. There was no particular criteria as to whose name was added to a memorial. It was simply down to those responsible for raising the money to determine how that would be achieved.

It wasn't as easy a process as one might think. It wasn't unusual for a man to appear on more than one local memorial. Inclusion could be down to an individual having been born in the town, or if not born there, having lived there immediately before going off to war. Some families moved away after their son, father, uncle or brother had been killed, so which memorial did their name appear on, the town in which they were born, where they had lived before the war or the town where their family had moved to after their death?

Sometimes a man's name would be spelt correctly on one memorial and then incorrectly on another. Some were known by nicknames which added to the confusion. By way of example a man with the name of say 'David White' might have been universally known by friends and family alike as 'Chalky'. His name would then be recorded on a war memorial as C. White rather than D. White, potentially causing havoc and mayhem years later for historians researching their name.

On each of the war memorial listings we have copied each of the names as they appear on the memorial on which they are commemorated. Hopefully we have recorded them correctly. If we have failed to do so or have inadvertently omitted someone's name, then we apologise.

For each memorial we have selected a number of names at random as well as others who we thought might have a particular story that would be good to look at in a bit more detail. Each and every one of those named on these memorials has their own individual story.

Aveley War Memorial

Aveley War Memorial is right in the centre of the town's main High Street. It is situated at the entrance to St Nicholas Church, which sits peacefully in the background. If you drive past too quickly, the memorial can be quite easily missed.

In the early 1920s when the war memorial was first erected the pace of life would have been much slower and vehicular traffic passing through Aveley High Street wouldn't have been at anywhere near the levels of today. Aveley was no more than a quaint little village where everybody knew everybody else, as well as each other's business. It was a time when young children could play in the street without worry and all they had to be mindful of was somebody riding past too fast on a bicycle or a runaway horse.

The war memorial in Aveley still sits proudly in the middle of the High Street so that anyone passing by can clearly see the names of those from the community who gave their lives in the Great War. Their names are like a beacon of a bygone era.

Below are the names of those who are commemorated on the

memorial:

C. Harkness	W. Skilton	E. Wade
S. Groves	J.Williams	D. Haslem
T. Morris	R. Pavitt	A. Riley
J. Cox	A. Childs	H. Wall
J. Plumridge	F. Rumble	A. Barker
W. Sewell	A. Southgate	P. Nunn
H.Willis	H. Richardson	J. Tyler
J. Smith	E. Flanders	E. Bright
H. Rumble.	V. Skilton	G. Watts
C. Kettle	A. Bunn.	S. Waight
G. Downs	A. Hunwick	H. Cook.
S. Thorogood	W. Farrow	T. Bond
F. Hunwick	D. Carson	H. Morris
J. Pavitt	J. Theedom	H. Rose

The names of forty-two men are recorded on the memorial. We will look at a few of them in more detail. The choice of those selected is purely random.

J. Theedom is John Frederick Theedom and he is recorded on two local memorials, the one at Aveley as well as the one at Horndon-on-the-Hill. At first glance it is not obvious why this is so, but on closer examination things become a little clearer.

Private **John Frederick Theedom** (71536) originally enlisted in the Essex Regiment (12367) before transferring to become a member of 35th Company, 23rd Machine Gun Corps (Infantry).

The 1911 census shows a home address of Belhus Park, Aveley, although he had been born at nearby Canvey Island. On the CWGC website, the details of which were first collated in 1921, the family's home address is shown as 8 Pump Street, Horndon-on-the-Hill, Stanford-le-Hope, Essex.

He was 23 years old when he was killed and is commemorated on the Cambrai War Memorial in Louverval, France.

The Aveley War Memorial clearly shows a J. and R. Pavitt, but when searching the CWGC website there are only four men with the name Pavitt and none of them has a Christian name that begins with the letter R. In fact all four of them have Christian names which begin with the letter J, so there must be an error on the memorial. This is what we found.

James Pavitt (41099) was a private in the 2nd Battalion, the Essex Regiment and was aged 37 when he was killed on 3 May 1917. His name is commemorated on the Arras War Memorial in the Pas de Calais.

According to the Commonwealth War Graves Commission, his parents, Robert and Lydia Pavitt, lived in South Ockendon and his wife, Ella May Pavitt lived at 67 Kenneth Road, Chadwell Heath, Essex, although in the 1911 Census James and Ella lived at 25 West Street, South Ockendon. They had a 5-year-old son named Ernest James Pavitt and a year old daughter, Hilda Mary Pavitt.

Before enlisting in the Army James's occupation is shown as a clerk, farmer and miller.

John Henry Pavitt (251661) was a lance corporal in the 20th Battalion of the Durham Light Infantry, although he had previously been a private (10390) in the East Surrey Regiment. He was 26 years old when he was killed on 23 March 1918. His name is commemorated on the Arras War Memorial.

His parents, Harry and Clara Jane Pavitt, lived at Lennards Cottage, High Steet, Aveley, Essex. The 1911 Census however, shows them as living at 1 Primrose Cottage, Romford Road, Aveley, Purfleet, Essex.

John Henry Pavitt was married when he was killed, but after the war his wife remarried, becoming Mrs B.A. Moore and moving to 58 Newton Road, Rushden, Northants.

When John Henry Pavitt enlisted in the army on 6 December 1915, he was living at 3 Belmont Road, Grays, Essex, he was 23 years old and his occupation was shown as a painter and decorator.

Herbert William Rumble (G/44034) was a private in 'D' Company, 17th Battalion of the Middlesex Regiment when he was killed on 12 November 1916. He was 36 years old. His mother, Sarah Ann Rumble lived in High Street, Aveley, Essex, which close to where the town's war memorial was subsequently placed.

The 1911 Census shows that Herbert had two brothers, Stephen (25), and Ernest (18), Neither of them are shown as having served in the military.

Having checked the CWGC website, there are three F. Rumbles, one of whom was in the Canadian Infantry, one was a gunner in the Royal Field Artillery and whose family lived in Holloway in London, the third is shown as being F.J. Rumble of the 1st Battalion, the Essex Regiment who was killed on 6 August 1915 and is buried in the Twelve Trees Cemetery in Turkey, indicating that he was killed during the Gallipoli Campaign. There is no family information recorded for him.

Searching the 1911 Census there is a Fred Rumble shown as living at 6 Ivy Row, High Street, Aveley, Essex. He was 14 years old. If F.J. Rumble and Fred Rumble are one and the same person, it would mean he would have been between 18 and 19 years of age at the time of his death.

William Frederick Skilton (5/4647) was a rifleman in the 1st Battalion, the King's Royal Rifle Corps. He was aged 22 when he was killed on 23 May 1916. He is buried along with 249 of his colleagues in the Zouave Valley Cemetery, Souchez, in the Pas-de-Calais.

His parents, Joseph and Ellen Harriet Skilton, lived at 5 Alms Houses, Aveley, Essex. William had one brother, Charles Henry Skilton (15) and a sister, Ellen Mary Skipton (19). William's brother Charles also served during the First World War and survived. He was a private (45656/8989) in the 2nd Battalion the Northamptonshire Regiment and enlisted when he was 19 years old on 9 March 1915 at Warley, his birthday being 21 January 1896. Before enlisting in the army, he was a labourer. His service record shows that he was only 5 feet 2 inches tall and weighed 8 stone 4 pounds and he had a 35-inch chest.

He served in France between 1915 and 1916 with the British Expeditionary Force before being wounded on 10 July 1916 with four gunshot wounds to his head and chest. On 23 July he was seriously ill in hospital in France and because of his condition he was sent back to England. He was awarded the British War Medal and the Victoria Medal on 11 September 1921.

Bulphan War Memorial
The war memorial is in the graveyard of St Mary the Virgin Church in the village of Bulphan. As you go through the gate at the front of the

Bulphan War Memorial.
(Stephen Wynn)

St Mary the Virgin Church (Stephen Wynn)

church, it stands slightly off to the left and is a cross of polished granite on an octagonal plinth that sits on a small concrete base.

The inscription on the memorial reads:

> *'To the glory of God and in gratitude to our sons and brothers who laid down their lives for their King and country in the Great War. Grant them eternal rest and let light perpetual shine upon them.'*

There are only twelve names recorded on the Bulphan War Memorial of those who lost their lives during the First World War. They are as follows:

William Edward Garrod (44030) was a private in the 10th Battalion, the Essex Regiment when he was killed on 24 August 1918, aged 19. He was the son of Mrs Kate E. Garrod of 2 Hall Cottages, Church Road, Langdon Hills, Essex, although he was born in Aveley. He is buried at the Bécourt Military Cemetery, Bécordel-Bécourt, France. He had previously been a private in the Bedfordshire Regiment before transferring to the Essex Regiment.

The 1911 Census shows William as living with both his mother and father, Kate Elizabeth and Ernest Garrod who were both aged 36, as well as his five brothers and sisters. In 1911 William was only 11 years old. On the CWGC website William's father, Ernest, is not shown, which suggests he passed away at a comparatively young age. His name appears on the Roll of Honour in St Mary's Church at Langdon Hills.

Arthur Albert Harrod (G/21493) was a private in 11th Battallion, The Queen's (Royal West Surrey) Regiment when he was killed on 8 October 1916. He was 21 years old. He is commemorated on the Thiepval Memorial on the Somme. He was the son of Harry and Emily Harrod of North Ockendon, Romford in Essex.

Jesse Hopkins Jones. On the 1911 Census there is only one person shown with this name. He was 25 years old and married to Ann Jones, with whom he had a one-year-old son, Jesse Morgan Jones.

Jesse was born in St Pancras in London and was a self-employed dairyman, living at 59 Tyas Road, Hermit Road, Canning Town, London.

A further search on Ancestry.co.uk, shows a person of the same name who was also born in St Pancras, London. He was a lance corporal in the 2nd Battalion, the Royal Welsh Fusiliers (17145) and died in France of his wounds on 8 March 1917.

S. Lambert (2300) was a private in the 2nd/19th Battalion of the London Regiment when he was killed on 18 August 1916, aged 21. He is buried in the Aubigny Communal Cemetery in the Pas de Calais. He was the son of James and Eliza Lambert of 'Westwood', Roughton, Norwich, Norfolk.

Arthur T. Jiggins (291537). Although the spelling on the war memorial at Bulphan is 'Jiggins', on the CWGC website the surname is shown as 'Jiggens'. He was killed on 6 October 1917 and was a private in the 2nd/7th Battalion of the Northumberland Fusiliers. He was aged 26 and is buried in the Cairo War Memorial Cemetery, at Al Qahirah, Egypt.

His parents, Charles Thomas and Julia Jiggens lived at Bulphan Fen, Essex.

To add to the confusion, when researching the same name in the military section of Ancestry.co.uk it comes up as Arthur Thomas Jiggins who was born in Dunton near Laindon. He enlisted at Woolwich in London, originally in the 1st/7th Battalion of the Northumberland Fusiliers. On the same website, but this time looking through the 1911 Census, the surname is spelt 'Jiggens'. Arthur had two brothers, Charles and Frederick as well as two sisters, Amelia and Olive.

On the 'International Find a Grave Index' on (www.findagrave. com) the spelling of the surname once again reverts back to 'Jiggens'.

This is another example of the difficulties involved in researching names from the past!

James Marsh was a rifleman (S/37278) in 'A' Company, 2nd Battalion, The Rifle Brigade when he died on 28 May 1918. He was 31 years of age and is commemorated on the Soissons War Memorial in the Aisne region of France.

Soissons War Memorial (Commonwealth War Graves Commission)

He was the son of the late Alfred and Emma Marsh. His wife, Rosa May Marsh, lived at 1 Cliff Cottages, Billet Lane, Leigh-on-Sea, Essex. On the 1911 Census James and Rosa are showing as living at 3 Barracks Lane, Rochford, Essex, James is shown as a 'platelayer' by way of occupation and they had four children, Ruby Rose May (6), Cecil Stanley (4), Lawrence Norman (3) and Horace Francis (1).

Sydney J Woollings (163273) was a private in the 75th Battalion of the Canadian Infantry Regiment. He was killed on 14 September 1916 and is buried in the Ridge Wood Military Cemetery in the West Flanders region of Belgium.

James Murray (251339) was a corporal in the 5th Battalion of the Essex Regiment when he was killed on 26 March 1917. There is some discrepancy on the actual date of his death as the CWGC website shows 26 March 1917 whilst the war memorial in Bulphan shows 27 March 1917. His name is commemorated on the Jerusalem War Memorial.

The following is taken from the CWGC website and is an historical description of the military situation in Jerusalem throughout the war

Jerusalem War Memorial (Commonwealth War Graves Commission)

whilst at the same time putting into context just how sustained the fighting was in this theatre of war, where James Murray lost his life,

'At the outbreak of the First World War, Palestine, which is now Israel, was part of the Turkish Empire and it was not entered by Allied forces until December 1916. The advance to Jerusalem took a further year, but from 1914 to December 1917, about 250 Commonwealth prisoners of war were buried in the German and Anglo-German cemeteries of the city.

By 21 November 1917, the Egyptian Expeditionary Force had gained a line about 5 kilometres west of Jerusalem, but the city was deliberately spared bombardment and direct attack. Very severe fighting followed, lasting until the evening of 8 December, when the 53rd Welsh Division on the south, and the 60th London and 74th Yeomanry Divisions on the west, had captured all the city's prepared defences. Turkish forces left Jerusalem throughout that night and in the morning of 9 December, the Mayor came to the Allied lines with the Turkish Governor's letter of surrender. Jerusalem was occupied that day and on 11 December, General Allenby formerly entered the city followed by representatives of France and Italy.

Meanwhile, the 60th Division pushed across the road to Nablus, and the 53rd across the eastern road. From 26 to 30 December, severe fighting took place to the north and east of the city but it remained in Allied hands.'

Arthur Henry William Stowell (80785) was a trumpeter in 'B' Squadron of the Essex Yeomanry, which was part of the Household Cavalry and Cavalry of the Line.

He died on 11 April 1917 at Monchy-le-Preux. He was 20 years old and is buried at the Feuchy Chapel British Cemetery in Wancourt in the Pas de Calais. Wancourt was captured from the Germans the day after Trumpeter Stowell was killed.

His father, also Arthur, lived at Glenmore, Bulphan, Essex.

There are 834 graves at the cemetery. At the time of the Armistice that number was only 249 but after the fighting had stopped those who had died on nearby battlefields, were reburied at Wancourt.

Feuchy Chapel British Cemetery (Commonwealth War Graves Commission)

Loos War Memorial (Commonwealth War Graves Commission)

James Graves (8635) was a private in the 2nd Battalion of the Highland Light Infantry when he was killed in action on 25 September 1915 at Givenchy. He was 36 years old at the time of his death. He is commemorated on the Loos War Memorial in the Pas de Calais.

His parents, John and Edith Graves lived at Manor Cottages, Bulphan in Essex. His wife, Kate Edith Graves lived at 25 Charles Street, Bridge Road, Grays, Essex. James's brother, Frederick, was also killed during the First World War.

Frederick Graves (1078) was a private in the 7th Battalion, the Australian AIF when he was killed on 8 May 1915 after landing on the west coast of the Gallipoli peninsula at Gaba Tepe, an area known as Anzac Cove. He was 27 years old and is commemorated on the Helles War Memorial in Turkey.

Helles War Memorial (Commonwealth War Graves Commission)

St Sever Cemetery (Commonwealth War Graves Commission)

George Stanway Jarvis (10808) was a private in the 1st Company, 3rd Battalion, the Royal Fusiliers when he was killed 10 October 1915. He was 32 years old at the time of his death and he is buried at the St Sever Cemetery in Rouen, France.

Frederick A.W. Cray (Essex Regiment) and Sydney A. Hammond are both shown on the war memorial, but we have been unable to find them on either the CWGC website or ancestry.co.uk.

Chadwell-St-Mary War Memorial

There are eight names recorded on the Chadwell-St-Mary war memorial of those who were killed from the area during the First World War. They are:

R.C. Ellis	W. Merchant
E. Gower	C. Turner
A. Hornsby	R.R. Wells
L. Littlechild	J. Young

In addition to these there are another six men who are buried in the graveyard at St Mary's Church who fell in the First World War, but for some unknown reason have not been included on the Chadwell-St-Mary War Memorial.

Stanley Ansell, served with the Royal Marine Light Infantry. His service number was CH/16575. He was discharged as a pensioner who had been invalided out of the army on 2 January 1918 due to pulmonary tuberculosis and subsequently died at home on 18 December 1919, aged 28.

He was the son of William and Sarah Ann Ansell of 8 Ottowa Road, Chadwell St Mary, Tilbury. According to the 1901 Census, his father had been born in Edmonton, north London and his mother in Childerditch, a hamlet some 10 miles north of Tilbury. Stanley was born at Leigh-on-Sea, Essex, as was his older brother William. He also had a younger sister, Ellen, who was born in Tilbury.

By the time of the 1911 Census Stanley was no longer living at home. He had joined the Royal Marines and was stationed at their barracks in Chatham in Kent.

His name is recorded on both the Little Thurrock war memorial where his middle initial is shown as being 'H' and the Tilbury War Memorial where he is simply shown as Ansell S.

Stanley is shown on the CWGC website and at the bottom of the entry against his name is the following: *'This casualty was accepted by the Commission recently. Special memorial headstone engraved, "Buried Elsewhere in this Churchyard" will now be placed near the entrance to the Churchyard.'*

Frederick James Baker was a bombardier (31474) with the Royal Garrison Artillery, when he died at home in Faversham in Kent on 27 October 1916, aged 29. He is buried at St Mary's Church in Chadwell-St-Mary in Essex. His parents were George James and Caroline Elizabeth Baker.

Henry Woodbury Bugler (M/12618) was a writer, 3rd Class in the Royal Navy and he was serving on HMS *Pembroke*, when he was killed on 11 April 1915. He was only 19 years of age. He is buried in the churchyard at St Mary's Church in Chadwell-St-Mary in Essex and his parents, Arthur and Elizabeth Bugler, are shown as living at 185 Burges Road, East Ham in London, so it is not known why Henry was then buried at Chadwell-St-Mary.

Ernest Gower (12649) was a lance corporal in the 9th Battalion the Essex Regiment when he was killed on 3 July 1916, aged 20. He is commemorated on the Thiepval War Memorial in France. His parents were Alfred and Jane Rebecca Gower and they lived at Court Farm, Aveley, Purfleet in Essex.

A. Hornsby (G/30620) was a private in the 10th Battalion of the Queen's Own Royal West Kent Regiment, when he was killed on 8 May 1918. He was 28 years of age and is buried in the Gwalia Cemetery in West Flanders, Belgium. His parents, Charles and Emma Hornsby, lived at Biggen Heath Cottage, Chadwell-St-Mary, Grays, Essex.

Grays War Memorial

Memorial building came of age after the end of the First World War. During 1920 and 1921 hardly a town or village across the entire country didn't have some kind of War Memorial erected to honour and remember local men who had lost their lives during the Great War.

The Grays war memorial, which was built by a local firm Marshal & Wilson, is also now classified as a listed building. It was unveiled to the public on 6 March 1921 and has remained in its original position ever since, thankfully never having been moved to accommodate a town centre shopping centre or a new-fangled inner ring road, as has happened elsewhere. It's still to be found at the north end of the High Street opposite the local Magistrates Court and it is an impressive monument by any standards, standing some 30 feet in height. Made of Portland stone, it stands on a double stone plinth which in turn sits on a concrete base surrounded by a decorative low metal railing.

Grays War Memorial (Pete Kittle)

The names of the dead are inscribed on copper plaques that adorn the east and west sides of the monument. The plaque on the south side carries the following inscription.

'This monument is erected in the year 1920 by the grateful inhabitants of Grays to the immortal memory of their brave fellow townsmen who answering the call of duty, left home and kindred in order to defend the empire and the cause of justice and especially to those whose names are inscribed on these tablets, who lost their lives whilst serving in the armed forces of the crown or in the Mercantile Marine during the Great War of 1914-1918.'

Further inscribed under this inscription is another in italics, it reads as follows.

'On fame's eternal camping ground their silent tents are spread and glory guards, with solemn round, this bivouac of the dead.'

There are 309 names on the memorial of men who were either killed or missing and never found, from the First World War. Each one of them is recorded below.

Abbott A T.	Beard P.J.	Bullock W.J.
Abrams W C.	Beckwith C.E.	Butler A.L.
Aldwinckle H.	Beeney S.L.	Byron A.
Ambrose F.B.	Benson J.	Campion C.P.
Aslett H.C.	Bestall E.D.	Capron T.H.O.
Anios F.A.	Birch W.	Carnell J.
Babbs W.J.	Bishop A.	Carter C.W.
Bailey W.D.	Blesene J.W.	Chapman,A.E.
Baker A.E.	Boston E.W.H.	Chatting W.
Baker F.D.	Boston W.D.	Cheeseman W T.
Baker J.	Boyle H.	Choppen, L.T.
Baldwin H.H.	Brag A.S.	Clarke J.
Bannister S.J.	Brander,H.	Clarke W.J.
Barker W.W.	Brook F.	Claydon H.A.
Bartlett J.H.	Brook R.E.	Claydon W.J.
Barton F.	Brown R.	Clements W.
Barton L.	Browning C.J.	Cliffen C J.
Bayford W.P.	Broyd E. J.	Coker E.E.
Beadle E.	Bruce J.	Collins C.A.

Collins P.J.

Collis A.

Colmer J.G.

Coplestone F.L.

Cosby G.A.

Cottis G.I.

Cottis H.C.

Crabb A.

Crawley J.

Crooks B.D.

Crooks H.

Cuckow J.E.J.

Curtis W.J.

Daley F.W. (MM)

Daniels A.V.

Davies G.

Davis G.W.T.

Dennis A.H.

Dennis F.

Dissil F.

Dorner F.

Dorner W.

Driscoll S.G.

Dunn R.

Emberson F.H.

England C.J.

Evans D.

Facer F.W.

Fairholm A.

Faraway S.V.

Farr A.E.

Farr A.J.

Flack R.J.

Flemming A.

Gant W.

Gaylor E. J.

Gibbs H.P.

Giggins E.J.

Gill J.F.

Gilson F.

Gilson J.H.

Godman E.J.

Godman W.A.

Goldspring J.B.

Goodman J.

Goodrum R.W.

Gomer C E.

Goody A.

Gore R.C.

Gower J.W.

Graham D.

Graves J.

Green H.

Green W.E.

Grout,F.J.

Harding H.J.

Harrington P.

Harris, E

Harris S G.

Harris S H.

Harvey E.M.

Harvey E.P.

Harvey F.

Harvey P.P.

Herrington W.H.G

Heymer G.R.

Heymer W.E.

Hibbin P.A.

Hide H.

Hills J.W.

Hills T.

Hines H.

Hines H.J.

Hirst A.

Hobbs F.

Hole D.

Honey H.G.

Horncastle E.H.

Howes, A.

Howes H.

Huckle G.

Hudson E.J.

Hudson T.

Hughes A.H.

Hurst A.

Hurst F. (MM)

Hurst J.

Hyde W.F.

Ingle S.H.

Jackson H.

Jackson P.

Jaggard C.H.

Johnson A.G.

Jones A.

Jones C.

Jones E J.

Keeling O.J.

Kelly J.J.

Kemp S.S.J.

Kennedy J.

Kennedy W.

Keyes H.J.

King W.G.

Knight H.C.

Knights L.J.S.

Knowles A.E.

Knowles L.A. (MM)

Last A.H.

Last J.W.

Laybourn J.J.

Law A.T.

Leach F.

Lenihan W.

Lethby E.E.

Lewis C.W.	Polley W.H.	Smith I.N.
Lewis E.	Pontney G.	Smith P.W.
Lindsay R.J.	Pratt L.	Smith W.J.
Lindsay W.C.	Prentis S.T.	Smith W.T.
Linzell J.	Pryer A.T.	Smith W.T.
Long F.G.	Quiddington O.L.	Smithson C.W.
Lord S.	Ramsey R.C.	Sparks F.C.
Low F.	Rate R.A.	Stammers W.H.
Lowe W.D.	Ray A.G.	Stanley G.W.
Macdonald,A.	Rayment A.W. (MM)	Stanley T.J.
Maudlin C.	Rayment W.	Steer I.
Mears W.	Read W.	Stephenson A.
Michell D.R.	Redshaw H.	Stillaway,A.C.
Michell R.E.	Reed W.	Stillaway A.G.
Miller A.	Reeve F.	Stillaway W.
Mitcham C.C.	Richards T.	Stokes,H.J.
Mitchell H.C.	Richardson E.C.	Stone J.
Mitchell W.J.	Rous T.L.	Stone P.H.
Monk E.C.	Ross J.	Sutcliffe T.E.
Morgan D.G.	Rouse W.	Sutton T.W.
Morrell T.D.	Rowe H.	Tapsell T.
Neal B.	Rushen C.E.	Targett J.H.
Nicholls A.E.	Salmon F.J.	Tedman W.
North A.F.	Savage H.O.	Templer J.H.
Norton J.	Saxby G.	Thomas W.E.
Olsen C.	Sayer E.E.	Thorpe R.W.
Parker C.	Seabrooke A.	Tokeley F.W.
Parker F.	Scales W.T.	Tomkins R.E.
Parker H.	Scott A.W.	Tomkins S.
Pavitt H.E.	Shipman A.H.	Tooley W.
Paxman S.H.	Silverwood H.F.	Turner S.B.
Payne G.	Simpson W.G.	Twin A.S.
Pentecost L.D.	Sims J.H.	Tyler J.A.
Perfitt F.J.	Skilton V.A.	Tyler S.W.
Pettingill F.C.	Slattery D.V.	Tyrrell F.
Pitts G.H.	Smith F.W.	Vaughan C.F.F.
Pollard J.	Smith, H.H.	Wakefield A.J.
Polley F.C.	Smith H.S.	Wakefield J.S.

Waleing C.	White A.	Wilden G.H.
Walker A.G.	White H.	Wilson J.F.
Warren W.E.	White R.J.	Wilson R.J.
Warren W.G.	Whitehead J.	Wood A.W.
Warrington F.	Whiteley F.J.	Wood G.J.
Watkins W.C.	Whitwell A.C.	Woollard W.C.
Webb W.M.	Wiggins A.A.	Wordley A.W.L.
West F.W.	Wilden E J.	Wright W.S.

The casualties recorded include four winners of the Military Medal and quite a few sets of brothers, whom we will look at in more detail as an overall representation of all the names commemorated on the memorial.

There are a few anomalies, however, that need addressing. In Grays New Cemetery there are seventeen servicemen who fell in the First World War but only ten of them appear on the Grays memorial.

One of those buried there is Private 12358 **William Reid** of the 9th Battalion, the Essex Regiment. He was killed on 9 October 1916 aged 19. He was the son of Matilda Reid of 5 West Street, Old High Street, Grays Essex. He is not shown on the Grays War Memorial.

There are, however, a W. Read and a W. Reed on the memorial. It is quite possible that William Reid is one of the above, but as there are eighty-nine men named W. Read and eighty-four named W. Reed on the CWGC website, it is not really possible to clarify the situation.

There is an R.E. Tompkiss shown as being buried in the New Grays Cemetery. He is also not on the Grays war memorial. There is however an R.E. Tompkins there, but when checking the CWGC website for the same name, there is no trace of him. Maybe R.E. Tompkins and R.E. Tompkiss are one and the same person.

There are also an E.H. Garland, Francis Herbert Hotham, a J.J. Anger and an E.C. Dorman buried in the same cemetery, yet none of them are showing on the Grays memorial, although E.H. Garland is commemorated on the one at Little Thurrock.

One of the saddest stories from the Grays War Memorial is that of the **Stillaway brothers, William, Alfred and Arthur**. Their parents, Matilda and Alan Stillaway, lived at 17 Manor Road, Grays, Essex.

William, 37 years of age, was the first son to die. At the time his mother and father were living at Custom House in London, but his wife A.B. Stillaway, lived at 17 Charles Road, Grays, Essex.

He was a storekeeper on HMS *Clan McNaughton*, the armed merchant cruiser, which sank off the north coast of Ireland on 3 February 1915. It is unclear exactly what caused the sinking. Some theories suggest it might have struck a German mine, but it was a particularly stormy night with atrocious weather conditions, leading to the plausible suggestion that it sank due to nothing more sinister than the bad weather. All 261 crew on board, including William, were lost.

If that scenario wasn't sad enough, two and a half years later, Alan, a dock worker at Tilbury, and Matilda Stillaway, lost their other two sons, Arthur, who was only 17 years of age and Alfred who was 22. They were both killed on 7 September 1917, when the ship they were serving on, the SS *Minnehaha*, was hit by a torpedo fired from German U-boat *U-48* and sank within four minutes. Forty-three members of the crew, including Arthur and Alfred, were killed.

They had a fourth son, Albert, who would have been twenty-one at the outbreak of the war. It is assumed he joined up but as he is not to be found on the CWGC website it can also be assumed that he survived the war.

Anthony William Rayment, (5/151) was in the 2nd Battalion the Royal Fusiliers. He was killed on 27 October 1916. He has no known grave and is commemorated on the Thiepval Memorial on the Somme. He was awarded the Military Medal. There are 72,000 names recorded on the Thiepval Memorial, ninety per cent of whom were killed during the period between July and November 1916.

Less than six months later Anthony's younger brother, William Thomas Sutton Rayment, who was a private in the 52nd Battalion of the Queen's Royal Regiment (West Surrey), was killed on 2 April 1917. He was only 18 years of age. He is buried in the New Grays Cemetery. His parents were Henry and Eliza Rayment of Grays.

Frank Hurst, another winner of the Military Medal, was killed on 19 March 1918. He was a lance corporal in the 8th Battalion of the Seaforth Highlanders. He was 27 years of age at the time of his death. He is buried in the Faubourg d'Amiens cemetery in the Arras region of France.

His parents were John and Mary Hurst who lived at 100 New Road, Grays. His brother, **Arthur Hurst**, a rifleman with the 1st/15th Battalion of the London Regiment (Prince of Wales's Own Civil Service Rifles), was killed on 21 August 1918, aged 20, and is buried at the Corbie Communal Cemetery on the Somme. They had two other sons, John and Tom Hurst who, although both old enough to have served during the war, are not shown on the Grays War Memorial.

L.A. Knowles was also a winner of the Military Medal. He was a lance corporal in the 13th Battalion of the King's Royal Rifle Corps, when he was killed only a week before the end of the war on 4 November 1918. He is buried in the Ghissingnies British Cemetery in the Nord Region of France.

Frank Daley, the fourth soldier commemorated on the Grays War Memorial to win the Military Medal, was a sapper in D Company, 2nd Battalion of the Canadian Railway Troops, when he was killed 20 December 1918. He is buried in the Busigny Communal Cemetery in the Nord region of France. Although his parents, Michael and Margaret Daley were from New Hampshire in the USA, Frank was married to Elisabeth M. Daley who lived at 153 Cromwell Road, Grays.

Horndon-on-the-Hill War Memorial
In the grounds of St Peter and St Paul Church in Horndon-on-the-Hill, is the gravestone of **Gunner J. Barnard** of the Royal Horse Artillery who was killed on 18 June 1916, aged 24.

However, Gunner Barnard's name is not engraved on the war memorial on the other side of the churchyard, tucked away in a walled enclosure, which looks on to a narrow road leading off the High Street..

There is one other soldier from the First World War who is also buried in the churchyard, Private 240684 **John Windle Westwood** of 'D' Company, 5th Battalion, the Seaforth Highlanders (I Duke of Albany's Rossshire Buffs), attached to the Trench Mortar Battery. He had enlisted in Middlesex.

Only 20 years of age, he had been wounded whilst serving on the Western Front and was brought back to England where he died of his wounds on 8 April 1917. His parents George Samuel and Frances Jane Westwood lived at Horndon-on-the-Hill. His name was included on the war memorial.

Horndon-on-the-Hill War Memorial (Stephen Wynn)

The memorial is an 8-foot high cross and is made of granite. The names are engraved in the plinth at the bottom of it and unfortunately were hard to read as they were starting to fade. The inscription read as follows:

'To the glory of God and in honoured memory of the men of this village who fell in the Great War 1914 -1918. They died that we might live.'

These are the names of seventeen young men commemorated on the base of the cross, who fell during the First World War:

Alfred H. Willis	George Macklin
John Windle Westwood	James Laver
Arthur G. Tyler	James W. Layzell
Percy J. Tyler	Charles W. Archer
Arthur Raven	Arthur Evans
William Nunn	Frederick Giggens
George A. Reeve	John W. Graves
Frederick G. Mitchell	J.F. Theedom
Walter J. Mead	

Gunner J. Barnard's full name is Jack Barnard. The CWGC website shows that he was killed on 18 June 1916 whilst serving with 'P' Battery of the Royal Horse Artillery on the Western Front in France. He was 24 years of age. He was born in Great Burstead, near Billericay and his parents, Joseph Arthur and Eliza Ann Barnard lived at 24 Chelmsford Avenue, Southend-on- Sea, Essex, so it is not immediately obvious why Jack was buried at Horndon-on-the-Hill.

The 1911 Census states that his mother had already died by that time and that his father was 63 years of age. Jack was living with his father and other family members at the address in Southend.

There is a slight anomaly in that on the CWGC website he is shown as Jack Barnard and on the 1911 Census he is shown as Joseph, but it is definitely the same person, as both show the same address of 24

Headstone of Gunner Jack Barnard. (Stephen Wynn)

Chelmsford Avenue, Southend-on-Sea, Essex. His father is also called Joseph, so maybe Jack was a nickname to ensure there would be no confusion as to who the father was.

Here are more details on some of those commemorated on the memorial.

Percy James Tyler (46525) was a rifleman with the 3rd Battalion, The Rifle Brigade (The Prince Consort's Own) when he was killed on 12 October 1918, having just turned 18, less than a month before the end of the war. He enlisted at Grays and lived at Hill Side Cottages, Horndon-on-the-Hill with his mother Emma and his brother Frederick, who on the 1911 Census was only aged 6.

Charles Walter Archer was a private (G/21140) in the 7th Battalion, The Queen's (Royal West Surrey Regiment) when he was killed on 28 September 1916. When he enlisted at Warley in Essex he originally joined the Middlesex Regiment where his service number was 26999.

Walter J. Mead was a sapper (256512) in the Royal Engineers. He was killed on 24 August 1918 and is commemorated on the War Memorial at St Peter and Paul's Church at Horndon-on-the-Hill, although he is actually buried in the nearby town of Stanford-le-Hope at the St Margaret of Antioch Church, which is immediately opposite the town's own war memorial.

Little Thurrock War Memorial

Drive down Rectory Road from Blackshots roundabout in Grays and you are in the district of Little Thurrock. About 200 yards further on is a set of traffic lights and a crossroads with Chadwell Road.

As you approach the traffic lights, the war memorial is on the right-hand side, raised and slightly back from the road. There are forty-eight names commemorated on it; of these there are seven that also appear on the nearby memorial in Grays town centre.

Ansell S H.	Bullock W.J.	Dodge S.R.
Alexander A.W.H.	Clark H.H.	Emberson F.H.
Alexander R.H.	Collins T.	Evans T.
Baker C.W.	Collins T.H.	Garland E.H.
Blunden W.	Cooper W.A.	Gore R.C.
Bowen T.	Davey R.	Green W.E.
Bullock H.A.	Davis C.W.T.	Gwynne S.

Little Thurrock War Memorial (Stephen Wynn)

Hawkes B.

Hicks A.C.H.

Hicks E.E.

Holliman H.J.

Mann H.S.

Meen H.B.

Moore G.H.

Oats A.J.

Penticost L.L.D.

Richardson G.

Smith L.E.

Spanton R.W.

Spooner A.C.

Spooner A.

Tandy W.L.

Taylor E.G.

Taylor G.

Ward J.

Wheaton E.

Wilson A. Jackson H.

Wood A.W.

Wood A.

Wood C.

Wordley A.W.L.

Whitby H.J. F.

Long J.W.

We have looked at a few of the names in more detail to try and give some substance to what it was these young men did so that others might enjoy a better life. We have tried to make them more than just some fading names on a war memorial from a bygone era that some have forgotten about.

Bullock H.A. is Harry Albert Bullock (12088), a corporal in the 9th Battalion, the Essex Regiment, who was killed on 12 November 1916. He was just 20 years of age. He has no known grave and is remembered on the Thiepval Memorial, in the Somme region of France. His parents, Emily and John Bullock, lived at 9 Dock Road, Little Thurrock, Grays, Essex.

Bullock W.J. is William James Bullock (28780), a lance corporal in the 10th Battalion, the Essex Regiment. He was aged 32 when he was killed on 30 March 1918. He was married to Mary Bullock of 1 Clement Block Cottages, Broadway, Grays, Essex.

Leonard Denyer Pentecost (203344) was a private in the 2nd/4th Battalion, the Queen's Own (Royal West Kent Regiment) when he died on 28 March 1917. He had originally been wounded at the Battle of Gaza on 26 March 1917 before subsequently dying of his wounds, aged 26. He is buried in the Kantana War Memorial cemetery in Egypt.

His parents, Annie and George Pentecost, lived at 'St Winifred's', Bridge Road, Grays, Essex. On the Little Thurrock War Memorial his surname is incorrectly spelt as Penticost.

Alfred Charles Henry Hicks (330162) was a private in the 1st Battalion of the Cambridgeshire Regiment. He was 28 years of age when he was killed on 29 September 1917. He commemorated on the Tyne Cot War Memorial in West Flanders, Belgium. His mother, Ann Hicks, lived at 14 Rectory Road, Little Thurrock, Grays, Essex.

Ernest Edward Hicks (G/6000) was Alfred's cousin and although shown as living at the same address in the 1911 Census, the record doesn't clarify if he lived there permanently or if he was just visiting when the census was taken.

He was a private in the 7th Battalion Queen's (Royal West Surrey) Regiment when he was killed on 1 July 1916, the first day of the Battle of the Somme. He is commemorated on the Thiepval War Memorial.

A.W.H Alexander (LZ/697) was an able seaman in the Royal Naval Volunteer Reserve when he died on 28 June 1918. He is buried in the Knightsbridge Cemetery in Mesnil-Martinsart in the Somme region of France.

Frederick Harry Emberson (50906) was a 24-year-old private in the 2nd Battalion of the Manchester Regiment. He had previously been Private 28038 in the Norfolk Regiment. He died on 6 December 1917 and is buried at the Mendinghem Military Cemetery in Poperinghe, West Flanders, Belgium. His parents, Harry and Annie Rose Emberson, lived at Cemetery Lodge, Grays, Essex.

He had a younger brother, Reginald (13) and a sister, Daisy Rose (11).

On the 1911 Census Frederick was shown as being aged 17 and an apprentice grocer by trade. Although he was born in Middlesex and lived in Grays, he enlisted in Birmingham.

Orsett War Memorial

Orsett is a small community which has a 'picture post card' appeal. As you drive into the village from the Stanford Road, crossing over the busy A13 which runs from London in the west to Southend in the east, you are immediately enveloped by the surrounding countryside and aware that you are approaching a rural community.

The war memorial is situated in the centre of the village, just

Orsett War Memorial. (Stephen Wynn)

opposite the Whitmore Arms, set back off the road in a quiet corner. If you drive too fast, you will miss it. There are fifty-eight names inscribed on the Orsett War Memorial of those who lost their lives in the First World War.

These young men were called upon to serve their country in a time of need, like thousands upon thousands of others up and down the country. They didn't shirk that call or the responsibility which went with it and in doing so they paid the ultimate price.

Charles Britton
John E. Argent
Philip Brook
Edmund G. Barnard
John Clark
Alfred J. Coker
Thomas Crabb
William T. Galley
Lionel Clarence Deakin
James E. Garlard
Arthur Emery
Leonard W. Jubb
Robert W. Francis
Leonard A. Martin
Charles Gentry
Ronald W. Marven
James E. Giggins
Ivor F. Pead
Frank Giggins
Frederick E. Smith
William G. Giggins
George West
Arthur Gladwel
Neville H. Wood
Frederick Greer
Cedric Wright
Albert Greygoose
Thomas C. Wright
Albert E. Moseley

Norman E. Suchamore
Ernest G. Francis
Archibald S. Harrod
James Pacey
James Haynes
Joseph Pacey
Charles Hazelton
Edgar W. Ridgwell
Frederick P. Hindes
Thomas E. Russell
Frederick Jackson
Alan Sanders
Ernest Judd
Charles Shaw
James Lambert
William Stubbs
Charles Laver
James Southgate
Arthur F. Lilley
John Southgate
Harry Malin
Garnet Thornton
Edgar Morris
George Turner
Arthur Motherself
Bertie E. Whiting
Henry Mundey
D'Arcy Wright
Robert Orr

We have randomly selected a few of them to look at in more detail.

John Henry Clark, (40050) was a private in the 11th Battalion of the Essex Regiment. He was aged 35 when he was killed in action 15 October 1916, in Flanders. He was the son of the late Charles William and Susan Clark.

There are three with the name of Giggins. Frank and William

George Giggins who were brothers and James Edward. Let's look at all three in more detail

Our first port of call was the CWGC website. There is no one with the name of **James Edward Giggins** recorded as having being killed during, or as a direct result of, the First World War. We then checked the British Army medal rolls index cards 1914-1920, once again there was no trace of anyone of that name having been awarded medals for service during the First World War.

The 1911 Census shows a James Edward Giggins, aged 26, living at West Street, South Ockendon, Essex, with his wife, Elizabeth Giggins and their eleven-month-old daughter Rosetta.

James's inclusion on the Orsett War Memorial is somewhat of a conundrum.

William George Giggins (L/10852) was a sergeant in 4th Battalion, Middlesex Regiment. He was 28 years of age when he was killed in action on 29 September 1915. His name is recorded on the Menin Gate Memorial in Ypres. He was the son of James and Emma Giggins of The Bungalow, Baker Street, Orsett, Grays, Essex.

William's brother **Frank Giggins** (15933) was a private in the 2nd Battalion of the Essex Regiment. He was 22 years of age when he was killed in action on 24 May 1915. Like his brother William, Frank's name is also recorded on the Menin Gate Memorial in Ypres.

Losing one son must have been a painful experience for any parent, but to have lost two sons in the space of only four months must have been devastating.

Albert Greygoose (12640) was a lance corporal in the 2nd Battalion of the Essex Regiment. He was killed on 1 July 1916, the first day of the Battle of the Somme. He is buried at the Sucrerie Military Cemetery in Colincamps.

James Southgate lived at 43 Maple Road, Grays in Essex according to the 1911 Census. His parents were Harry and Elizabeth Southgate and he had two younger sisters, but what was surprising was that there was no John Southgate. We couldn't find a separate entry on the 1911 Census for a John Southgate living anywhere near Grays and neither could we make a direct match with the same name on the CWGC website.

Entering the name James Southgate in the CWGC website comes up with six possibilities, but even using a simple process of elimination it still leaves two strong possibilities for the James Southgate whose name is recorded on the Orsett War Memorial. Similarly, there are three John Southgates showing on the same website. It is possible to eliminate only one of them, so there are still two possibilities for John Southgate.

Arthur Motherself is an interesting case. We have researched the name on both the 1911 Census and the CWGC website and his name doesn't come up on either.

Joseph Woodley Pacey was a serjeant observer in 206 Squadron Royal Air Force. He was 21 years of age when he was killed on 29 July 1918. His mother, Eliza Maria Pacey, lived at 'St Winifred's', Pound Corner, Orsett, Grays, Essex. The 1911 Census shows Eliza, James and Joseph living in the 'Foxhound' Public House, High Street, Orsett.

Purfleet War Memorial
The names of twenty-five young men who lost their lives during the First World War are commemorated on the Purfleet War Memorial.

Gunner Charles F. Rogers
Private Dugald Campbell
Sapper Joseph J. Randall
Private Alfred J. Godfrey
Sapper Bertie E. Gathercole
Private John B. Goldspring
Private Reuben T.W. Beauman
Private Basil S. Johnson
Private Edward J. Mckay
Private George Newton
Private Arthur H. Reed
Private Charles Riches
Private Thomas W. Rowland
Private Archibibald J. Saich
Private John Suckling
Private Edgar L.Truelove
Private William G. Watkin
Chief Petty Officer John Northmore
Second Lieutenant William D. Scott
Serjeant George W. Clarke
Bombadier Harry H. Watkins
Bombadier Arthur F. Hills
Lance Corporal Sydney J. Biles
Lance Corporal John B. Conerly
Lance Corporal John Newbould

Purfleet War Memorial and (inset) plaque. (Stephen Wynn)

Once again here are details of some of those named on the memorial to give a flavour of the lives they led and the times that they lived in.

John Barrett Goldspring (19001) was a private in the 1st Battalion, the Coldstream Guards when he was killed on 15 May 1918 aged 34. In the spring of 1913 he was married to Hannah C. Buck and they lived in nearby Grays.

He is buried at the Bienvillers Military Cemetery in the Pas de Calais. The cemetery has 1,605 Commonwealth graves from the First World War. A staggering 425 of these are burials of unidentified individuals, which underlines just how bloody and brutal some of the fighting during the war was.

The 1911 Census shows him as living with his parents, John Barrett (senior) and Caroline Goldspring at 29 Northcote Road, Gravesend, Kent. Before enlisting in the army he was a crane driver on a coal wharf in Gravesend.

Although the war memorial shows **Bertie Gathercole** (58937) as a sapper, he was in fact a pioneer in the 9th Division Signal Company of the Royal Engineers. He was killed on 18 October 1915 aged 22. He is buried in the picturesquely named Railway Dugouts Burial Ground (Transport Farm) in what is now the Ieper (Ypres) region of Belgium.

Railway Dugouts Burial Ground. (Commonwealth War Graves Commission)

The 1911 Census shows Bertie Gathercole as having been born in Fambridge, Essex and living at 37 Paper Mill Cottages, Purfleet, Essex, with his parents, James and Annie Gathercole, his five sisters, Marion (20), Ella (16), Rosie (13), Doris (7) and Grace (4). Before enlisting in the Army, Bertie had been a general labourer at a paper mill, where he worked with his father. There is also a suggestion that he had the middle name of 'Aldred', although this is not shown on the hand written copy of the 1911 Census.

Archibald James Albert Saich (15987) was a private in the 1st Battalion, the Essex Regiment when he was killed on 6 August 1915. He is commemorated at the Helles War Memorial in Turkey.

The 1911 Census shows him as a cellar man at the Royal Hotel, which is situated just across the road from where the war memorial that has Archibald's name inscribed on it, stands. The Royal Hotel wasn't just his place of work but where he lived as well. He shared it with eight other people, none of whom he was related to.

Looking at the 1901 Census shows us that Archie was a 10-year-old boy living at home with his parents, James and Mary Saich, and five brothers, Frederick (23), Clement (14), William (12), Albert (8) and Robert (6). He also had two sisters, Laura (20), and Maud (2). Their address was 5 Hotel Square, Purfleet, perhaps not too far away from the Royal Hotel where Archibald ended up working ten years later.

When taking into account the ages of Archibald's brothers in 1901, it is inconceivable to believe that William, Albert and Robert didn't serve in the armed forces during the First World War, even though we have been unable to find any trace of them having done so.

William David Scott was a temporary second lieutenant in the 26th Battalion of the Royal Fusiliers (City of London Regiment) when he was killed on 3 August 1917. He is commemorated on the Menin Gate War Memorial at Ypres, Belgium as he has no known grave.

The following is taken from the historical notes contained within the CWGC website about the Ypres Menin Gate War Memorial.

'The Menin Gate is one of four memorials which commemorates those missing in action as a result of the fighting during the First World War in Belgian Flanders.

Menin Gate Memorial. (Commonwealth War Graves Commission)

The Ypres Salient was formed during the First Battle of Ypres in October and November 1914, when a small British Expeditionary Force succeeded in securing the town, pushing the German forces back to the Passchendaele Ridge. The Second Battle of Ypres began just six months later in April 1915 when the Germans released poison gas into the Allied lines just north of Ypres. This was the first time gas had been used by either side, and the violence of the attack forced an Allied withdrawal.

The third Battle of Ypres in 1917, took place when Commonwealth forces mounted an offensive to divert German attention from a weakened French front further south. The initial attempt in June to dislodge the Germans from the Messines Ridge worked and was a complete success, but the main assault north-eastward, which began at the end of July, quickly became a struggle against a determined opposition and the rapidly *deteriorating weather. The campaign finally came to a close in November 1917 with the capture of Passchendaele.*

The battles of the Ypres Salient claimed many lives on both sides and it quickly became clear that the commemoration of members of the Commonwealth forces with no known grave could not be recorded at just one location.

The site of the Menin Gate was chosen because of the hundreds of thousands of Allied soldiers who passed through it on their way to the battlefields. It commemorates casualties from the forces of Australia, Canada, India, South Africa and United Kingdom who died in the Ypres Salient and who have no known grave; in the case of British casualties, only those who were killed prior 16 August 1917, with some exceptions. United Kingdom and New Zealand servicemen who died after that date are named on the memorial at Tyne Cot, a site which marks the furthest point reached by Commonwealth forces in Belgium until nearly the end of the war. New Zealand casualties who died prior to 16 August 1917 are commemorated on memorials at Buttes New British Cemetery and Messines Ridge British Cemetery.

The Ypres Menin Gate Memorial now bears the names of more than 54,000 officers and men. The memorial was unveiled by Lord Plumer on 24 July 1927.'

Edgar Lewis Truelove (15985) was a private in the 9th Battalion, the Essex Regiment when he was killed on 19 September 1917; he was 24 years of age. He is buried at the Monchy British Cemetery at Monchy-le-Preux.

His parents, William and Clara Emily Truelove, lived at 4 Station Terrace, Purfleet, Essex. In the 1911 Census the family is shown as living at 112 Tooley Street, Bermondsey. Edgar was then 17 years of age and was a waterman's apprentice. He had older two sisters, Eva (23) and Hilda (21). His brother William was two years older than him.

South Ockendon War Memorial
The War Memorial in South Ockendon sits on the edge of the village green; its backdrop is the seventeenth century Royal Oak public house and the unusually designed St Nicholas Church with its unique Norman tower.

Monchy British Cemetery. (Commonwealth War Graves Commission)

South Ockendon War Memorial with detail of inscription. (Stephen Wynn)

ERECTED
IN EVER GRATEFUL
MEMORY OF
THE MEN OF THIS PARISH
WHO FELL
IN THE GREAT WAR
1914 – 1918

"THEIR NAME LIVETH
FOR EVERMORE"

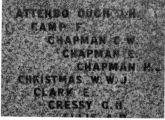

ATTENBO OUCH J.H.
CAMP F.
CHAPMAN C.W.
CHAPMAN E.
CHAPMAN H.J.
CHRISTMAS W.W.J
CLARK E.
CRESSY G.H.

Inscription of Attenbo Ouch.

It was already a village before the Norman Conquest and first had its own church as far back as 1085. It is mentioned in the Domesday Book as Wokenduna, supposedly named after a Saxon Chief named Wocca, whose tribe lived on a hill. A low hill in old English was called a 'don'.

The names of the forty-three young men from the parish who lost their lives during the First World War are all commemorated on the memorial.

Attenbo Ouch J H.	Kemp C.W.	Plume W.
Camp F.	Knopp F.	Richardson H.H.
Chapman C.W.	Knopp W.	Saville J.
Chapman E.	Lake B.	Sills L.
Chapman H.J.	Lake F.J.	Smith F.E.
Christmas W.W.J.	Lark A.	Smith G.
Clark E.	Mansfield T.	Spicer C.
Cressy G.H.	Marchant F.J.	Stowers A.C.
Ellis A.R.	Marshall E.J.	Upson F.
Giggins J.E.	Newborn D.	White R.
Giggins T.	Oakley T.B.	Willingham A.
Giggins W.	Palmer E.	Willis A.H.
Gilbey P.	Pavitt J.	Willis S.
Gilbey W.	Player J.	
Hawkins W.	Plume G.H.	

Frederick James Lake (58773) was a saddler in the 52nd Battery Royal Field Artillery when he died on 26 August 1914. He is commemorated on the La Ferté-Sous-Jouarre Memorial in the Seine-et-Marne region of France. The cemetery commemorates some 3,740 officers and men of the British Expeditionary Force who fell at the battles of Mons, Le Cateau, the Marne and the Aisne between the end of August and early October 1914, and who have no known graves.

There is some confusion round the three entries for the name Giggins on the South Ockendon war memorial because there are also three entries on the Orsett war memorial. W. and J.E. Giggins are commemorated on both and we have not been able to find a T. Giggins, so we have to wonder if that's not simply a misspelling of F. Giggins.

On the balance of probabilities, we would suggest that the three Giggins who are recorded on the South Ockendon war memorial are the same ones who are commemorated on the Orsett war memorial. Yet again, a clear example of how easy it is for confusion to reign in these matters and how everything can turn on a different initial or the different spelling of a surname.

Arthur Willingham (30685) was a lance corporal in the 4th Battalion of the Bedfordshire Regiment when he died on 30 October 1917. He is commemorated on the Tyne Cot War Memorial in Zonnebeke, Belgium.

When searching for Arthur on the CWGC's website only two possible individuals come up. One is an Albert and he is buried in Gillingham in Kent, so that only leaves the other who was in the Bedfordshire Regiment.

When we then checked the same details on the Ancestry.co.uk website, the same individual is shown as Arthur Lionel Willingham, a resident of Flitton in Bedfordshire, so we cannot positively confirm that these details relate to those recorded on the South Ockendon war memorial.

Stanford-le-Hope War Memorial
The war memorial in Stanford-le-Hope sits proudly in the middle of the town, a silent witness to a bygone era. The names of eighty-three young men from the parish are recorded on the memorial as having lost their lives during the First World War. The memorial was unveiled on 28 September 1920 by local dignitaries at a cost of £741, which was raised by local parishioners, an estimated 3,000 of whom turned out for the unveiling.

The memorial is in the shape of an obelisk which is made of Portland stone with the name tablets of a contrasting red granite. It stands at the top of the High Street, immediately opposite the St Margaret of Antioch Church.

The names of those recorded on the memorial, are as follows.

H. Myall	P.J. Nevard	J.W. Nichols
S. Sullings	D.J. Tween	E. Wade
H.C. Nash	J. Tween	E. Noakes

Stanford-le-Hope War Memorial. (Stephen Wynn)

F.S. Warren	F. Mitchell	W.T. Smith
D. Norman	A.J. Smidmore	D.D. Spall
V. Watt	H.V. Eaton	S.C. Spooner
T.L. Packman	W.J. Frost	C. Squire
G. Weald	A.T. Garwood	A. Styles
J.C. Page	E.F. Garwood	H. Attwater
A.Webster	A. Gladwell	E. Aves
T.S. Page	G.E. Greenaway	A.H. Bakewell
W.A. West	S.W. Greenwood	J.E. Bakewell
A.E. Parnell	H.Handscombe	J.E. Banks
G. Whybro	E.W. Hawkins	E.J. Bearman
L.W. Parren	B. Haxell	S.H. Bearman
F.Wilsher	S. Hockley	C.C. Bettis
J.E. Wilsher	A. Horlock	P. Brewster
J. Dobson	F. Jennings	F. Bridger
H. Wood	W.F. Jiggins	E.J. Britton
F.J. Dann	B. Jordon	H. Calderbank
A. Savill	O. Keeling	T. Challis
L.Wright	C. Ketley	E. Cook
G. Seaman	H.W. Lester	H.H. Cooke
J. Mann	E. Loury	F. Cox
G. Shead	P. Loury	T.G. Cox
E. Marshall	C.F. Greenwood	H. Crickmer
A.G. Shelley	H.D. Smith	J.G. Crickmer

From time to time a name will come up on a war memorial that throws up an anomaly. The name in question on this occasion is **Ernest Noakes**. He was a son of the town having been born in Stanford-le-Hope on 12 September 1891.

His parents, Eliza and Walter Noakes, had seven other children besides Ernest, four older sons and three younger daughters. All four of Ernest's brothers, William, Christopher, Frederick and John were of the right age to have served in the First World War. Having checked on the CWGC website, none of the four brothers are recorded as having been casualties of the war. The anomaly in question is, neither is Ernest, despite his name appearing on the Stanford-le-Hope war memorial as having been killed.

Ernest enlisted in the Canadian Expeditionary Force in Toronto, Canada and became a gunner with the 1st Battery, 12 Brigade on 1 October 1915. The witness at his attestation ceremony was one of his sisters, Ethel, who by now was married and had moved to Canada and become Mrs Peacock. Ernest was eventually demobbed from the army on 9 May 1919.

The question as how and why his name came to be included on the memorial remains a mystery.

Situated immediately across the road from the Stanford-le-Hope war memorial is the St Margaret of Antioch Church. Amongst those who are buried the church's cemetery are the graves of six soldiers from the town who were killed during the First World War. They are James Edmund Banks, F. Jackson, Patrick Lowry, W.J Mead, George Weald, Alfred Willis and one from the Second World War, Leslie Alfred Latter.

The names of James Edmund Banks and Patrick Lowry (Loury) are recorded on the Stanford-le-Hope war memorial, but the other four names are not. Of those, we know that W.J. Mead is recorded on the war memorial at Horndon-on-the-Hill.

Out of all the six names, only Patrick Lowry (Loury) is recorded on either of the plaques located inside St Margaret's Church.

Seven names on the war memorial are not shown on either of the church plaques, but that becomes six when you take out the name of Ernest Noakes. They are: D. Norman, S. Sullings, V. Watt, D. Keeling, E. Marshall, A. Gladwell.

A check on the CWGC website shows ten names when you enter D. Norman. Only one of the ten is shown as having any direct connection to Essex and that is **Douglas Herbert Norman** (G/5508), a private with the 13th Battalion of the Royal Fusiliers, who died on 11 August 1916 aged 18. He is buried at Southend-on-Sea (Sutton Road) cemetery.

This is a strong indication that he was wounded whilst serving abroad and returned to the UK to have his wounds treated in a military hospital, but subsequently died.

His parents are shown as Mr and Mrs Norman of 'Acacia', 52 The Grove, Southend-on-Sea although on the 1911 Census the family are shown as living at 33 Guildford Road, Southend-on-Sea, Essex. Douglas had an elder brother, Ernest, as well as five sisters.

If Douglas Herbert Norman is the D. Norman commemorated on the Stanford-le-Hope war memorial, it is not immediately obvious why he has been recorded on it. Any connection with the town would appear to have been but a fleeting one and some years before he was killed during the First World War.

S. Sullings is **Stephen John Sullings** and what is remarkable about his story is that he was a priest with the Army Chaplains department, attached to the 54th East Anglian Division, Royal Army Medical Corps.

He held the rank of Chaplain 4th Class. In the 1911 Census he is shown as living at number 81 Ormerod Road, Burnley, Lancashire. Stephen and his wife Edith had three children, a son Stephen (10), and two daughters Eva (13) and Winifred (5).

Stephen contracted malaria whilst serving in Egypt where he arrived in August 1915. He was returned to the UK and sent to the King's Norton Workhouse Infirmary, which during the First World War was used as a military hospital, for treatment and recuperation. It later became Selly Oak Hospital in Birmingham. Unfortunately Stephen did not recover from his illness and died in hospital on 21 November 1915.

Once again it would appear that his only connection with Stanford-le-Hope was that he was born in the town and spent his childhood years there. The 1881 Census certainly shows that he was living there as a 13-year-old schoolboy.

Remarkably his father, Thomas Sullings, who was a builder by trade, was still living at Westbourne Villas, Southend Road, in Stanford-le-Hope according to the 1911 Census, at the ripe old age of 82. He died in 1913 aged 84.

Stephen's brother Joseph, is also shown in the 1911 Census as living in the town at Westbourne House in Southend Road. Like his father, Joseph, was a builder and a contractor and lived with his wife, Alice, and their four children. Joseph's two sons, Ralph and Thomas both served in and survived the First World War. Thomas served as a private with the 4th London Regiment, the 3rd London Regiment and the East Surrey Regiment.

Ralph served in 13th London Regiment as a private and the Suffolk Regiment as a second lieutenant.

It would appear that the main reason why Stephen was commemorated on the town's war memorial was because, despite not having lived there for many years, he still had family members living in Stanford-le-Hope after the war.

V. Watt is commemorated on the Stanford-le-Hope war memorial, although he wasn't killed during the First World War, he survived it. He was taken prisoner by the Germans in October 1914 at the Battle of Mons and not released until after the war.

The 1911 Census shows the Watt family living at 119 Toronto Road, Tilbury in Essex. Andrew Thomas and Charlotte Elizabeth Watt lived there with their two sons **Victor George Watt**, aged 18, who had been born at Eastbourne in Sussex, Reginald A. Watt, aged 16, born at Stanford-le-Hope and their younger sister, Gladys Victoria, aged 13, and who was also born in Stanford-le-Hope.

Before the war the brothers both worked at the nearby Tilbury Docks as labourers.

When searching the CWGC website, there is no sign of Victor having been killed, which is already confirmed as we know that he was taken prisoner by the Germans in 1914, but unfortunately, Reginald wasn't so fortunate.

Reginald Alfred Watt (10881) was a private in the 2nd Battalion of the King's Own Yorkshire Light Infantry when he was killed on 6 November 1914, ironically in the same theatre of war and where Victor was taken prisoner only a matter of days beforehand. Reginald is buried at the Boulogne Eastern Cemetery in the Pas de Calais.

It would appear the inclusion of Victor Watt and the exclusion of Reginald Watt on the Stanford-le-Hope war memorial is down to nothing more sinister that a clerical oversight.

O. Keeling is **Oliver Joseph Keeling** (10539), a private in 9th Battalion, the Essex Regiment when he died on 19 March 1916, aged 21. He is buried at the Vermelles British Cemetery in the Pas de Calais region of France. He enlisted at the headquarters of the Essex Regiment, which was at Warley barracks on the outskirts of Brentwood.

His parents, Frederick James and Emily Jane Keeling lived at 14 Stifford Road, Grays, Essex. The reason for Oliver's inclusion on the Stanford-le-Hope war memorial is not an obvious one, as he was not a

Boulogne Eastern Cemetry. (Commonwealth War Graves Commission)

resident of the town, rather that of nearby Grays, on whose war memorial he is also commemorated.

As has been mentioned previously, there was no official criteria set down for how it was determined who should be included on a particular memorial. This was a local decision left to those who originally arranged and paid for the memorial's building and erection.

The 1911 Census shows that the Keeling family were living at 9 Angle Place, Angle Road, West Thurrock, Grays, Essex and that Oliver was born in Tilbury in 1894. Oliver, who was 17 years old at the time, had four brothers and a sister, Mary (22), Frederick (23), William (19), Walter (6) and Arthur (3). Prior to enlisting in the Army, Oliver, along with his two elder brothers, was a labourer at a local cement factory, while their father worked as a labourer at Tilbury Docks.

Frederick and William both served during the First World War and survived.

E. Marshall was **Edward Victor Marshall** (J/29949). The CWGC website shows that he was a Boy 1st Class in the Royal Navy and was serving on HMS *Formidable* at the time of his death on 1 January 1915. He was awarded the 1915 Star, the Victory Medal as well as the British War Medal. His body was never recovered and he is commemorated on the Portsmouth Naval Memorial.

HMS *Formidable* was a battleship that was first commissioned in 1901. In the early hours of New Year's Day 1915 she was sunk whilst on exercises 37 miles off the Devon coast by the German submarine, *U-24*, who dispatched two torpedoes into her hull to send her to the bottom of the sea.

The weather conditions couldn't have been much worse: high seas, coupled with strong winds and heavy rain. The stricken ship sank in less than two hours. Out of the crew of 750 men, 550 perished including the ship's commander, Captain Loxley, who made no attempt to escape his fate.

Although there was time to lower some of the ship's wooden life boats, a few of them didn't even make it into the water, instead they were smashed against the side of the ship, tossing those inside into a cold and watery grave. One of the lifeboats finally made it to shore after twenty-two hours of being battered and beaten by the worst the sea could throw at her. There were seventy-one crew on board, forty-eight of them had survived. Fourteen had died during the journey to safety, another six were found to be dead as they were removed from the lifeboat and three more died soon afterwards.

One of those who survived was Able Seaman Tom Walker. Due to injuries he received in the sinking of HMS *Formidable* he was discharged from the Royal Navy in April 1915 and declared 'medically unfit for naval service'. He received an 'honourable discharge' certificate which was signed personally by King George V, but this was not to be the end of his war. In 1917 he re-enlisted and this time joined the British Army and served in France. He served his country again during the Second World War both with the British Expeditionary Force and later as an Unexploded Bomb Disposal officer.

On the 1911 Census Edward Marshall was aged 13 and living at

Glen-Lyn, Branksome Avenue, Stanford-le-Hope, Essex, although he was actually born in Devizes, Wiltshire. His parents were Edward Walter John and Marion Marshall and he had an elder brother, Leonard (16), and a sister, Edith (17).

By the time of Edward's death his parents had moved to Lavender Gardens in Clapham, south-west, London. His brother **Leonard Marshall** (A1580) was a staff sergeant in the Army Ordnance Corps and survived the war. He was awarded the same medals as Edward. Leonard married Miss Ivy Doris Miriam Popham on 10 November 1917 at St James Church in Enfield in Middlesex.

A. Gladwell is **Arthur Gladwell** (129858). He was a pioneer in the Corps of Royal Engineers and had previously been a private (11386) in the 15th Battalion Special Brigade Royal Engineers of the 5th Middlesex Regiment. He was killed in action on 23 June 1916 and is commemorated on the Thiepval War Memorial. He was born in Stanford-le-Hope and enlisted in nearby Grays.

The 1911 Census shows a 14-year-old Arthur living at home with his family at Southfields Estate, Orsett, Grays, Essex. His father does not appear in the census and may well be dead, leaving just his mother Martha, to bring up Arthur, his sister Gertrude (19), James William (16) and John Robert (12).

James William Gladwell (21189) was aged 22 when he enlisted into the army. There is contradictory information recorded on his service record as to whether the date of his enlistment was 12 February 1916 or 12 February 1917. He signed on for the 'duration of the war' as a private in the 8th Battalion, the Royal West Kent Regiment. At the time he was living at Mucking Heath Farm in Orsett, one would imagine because that was also his place of work.

He was captured and taken prisoner at the Battle of Cambrai on 23 November 1918 and held at Munster II camp in Germany. He was finally released from captivity on 2 December 1918 and was repatriated to the UK on 10 December 1918, landing at Hull in the north-east of England. After this his home address was 5 Chimneys, Orsett Near Grays, Essex.

Reading through his army service record shows that while he was stationed at Maidstone, he was disciplined on 25 February 1919 for, *'breaking out of barracks after tattoo, remaining free until 10.15 on the 10th March'*. He was punished by forfeiting fourteen days' pay. If he had done the same whilst serving in France during the war, he would have no doubt faced a court martial and if found guilty, been shot for desertion in the face of the enemy, especially if it had been in the first few years of the war.

Steven John Cape wrote a book about Stanford-le-Hope's War Memorial. One of the names he mentioned from the memorial was Nevard P.J. We would respectfully suggest that the name recorded on there should have been Nevard H.P., for Harold Percival Nevard.

The CWGC shows a **Harold Percival Nevard** (10632), a private in the 9th Battalion, the Essex Regiment, who was killed on 3 July 1916, aged 21, just three days into the Battle of the Somme. He is commemorated on the Thiepval War Memorial. His parents were William John and Bertha Augusta Nevard of 148 Upper Bridge Road, Chelmsford, Essex.

On the 1911 Census William John and Bertha Augusta Nevard are living at an address in Corringham. They have two sons, one of whom is Harold Percival Nevard aged 15, which puts him at the correct age, allowing for the fact that he might not have had his sixteenth birthday until after the 1911 census had been taken.

When looking at the 1911 census records on Ancestry.co.uk for Henry Percival Nevard there is an option to click on his name under the heading, 'UK soldiers died in the Great War, 1914-1919'. This then shows the same date of death, the same service number and the fact that he was a member of the 9th Battalion, the Essex Regiment.

He landed in France with his regiment on 30 May 1915, so qualifying him to be awarded the 1915 Star along with the Victory medal and the British War medal.

Stifford Clays War Memorial
The War Memorial at Stifford Clays stands in the cemetery at St James Church, just as you enter the village of Stifford from the A13. There are thirty-one names commemorated on the memorial.

Bloomfield, John James
Bransden, Harold
Clack, William
Clayden, James

Crabb, Arthur Eric
Crabb, Arthur
Crow, George Frederick
Crow, Albert Charles

Stifford Clays War Memorial. (Stephen Wynn)

England, Albert John
Flook, Frederick William
Francis, Edwin John
Goodger, Harold
Graygoose, Albert
Hammond, David
Hills, Arthur
Mercer, Bertie
Hodges, William James George
Moore, William George
Bushell, Alfred
Ellmore, Alfred George

Vincent, William George
Lay, J.H
Packett, David
Parker, Harry Walter
Pavey, Charles
Payne, Fred Albert
Payne, Leonard
Payne, Ernest
Reeman, Frederick George
Reynolds, John Stevens
Wakefield, Amos

A search of the CWGC website shows only one entry for anyone with the surname Ellmore and that is for an Alfred Ernest Ellmore and not Alfred George, so we can only suggest that the initials shown on the war memorial are possibly incorrect as it would appear that we are talking about the same person.

Alfred Ernest Ellmore (44780) was a Sapper in 92nd Field Company, the Royal Engineers, when he was killed on 1 February 1917, aged 38. His wife is shown as Esther Kate Ellmore of 55 Toronto Road, Tilbury Docks, Essex.

He is buried in the Étaples Military Cemetery in the Pas de Calais region of France.

The following is an entry taken from the historical notes section on the CWGC website about the Étaples Military Cemetery which contains 10,771 Commonwealth burials from the First World War.

'During the First World War, the area around Etaples was the scene of immense concentrations of Commonwealth reinforcement camps and hospitals. In 1917, 100,000 troops were camped among the sand dunes and the hospitals which included eleven general, one stationary, four Red Cross hospitals and a convalescent depot which could deal with 22,000 wounded or sick.'

The 1911 Census shows an Alfred Ernest Ellmore living at 20 Globe Terrace in nearby Grays. This appears to have been the family home of John and Eliza Dawsett and their daughter, Clara Anne (13). Prior to joining the Army Alfred was employed as a labourer at Tilbury Docks.

In the 1901 Census he was living as a boarder at 38a St Anne Road, Barking, which is the town where he was born. The 1891 Census shows him living with his parents, John and Sarah Ellmore at the family home in Barking, along with his twin brother John, his elder sister Mary (22), and his younger brother George (9).

George Ellmore (8542) also served in the First World War as a gunner in the Royal Regiment of Artillery (Royal Garrison Artillery). He was not quite 20 years of age when he enlisted in the army on 14 August 1901 in London, originally for three years. On 1 April 1904 he extended this to eight years finally leaving the army on 13 August 1909. Exactly four years later on 14 August 1913, George re-joined the army, signing on for another four years.

On the 1911 Census George is shown as living with his elder brother John and his family in Middlesex where he was a postman.

He was one of the very first British troops to arrive in France on 16 August 1914. George was wounded on 10 April 1915 after which he then spent a period of time in hospital in Rouen before being discharged from there on 5 May 1915.

Unfortunately his service record isn't totally legible but we know he received a gunshot wound to the chest on 12 November 1917. He was sent back to England for treatment on 4 December 1917 where he spent a total of sixty-seven days in hospital, originally at Whipps Cross War Hospital in Leytonstone, before being transferred to a military hospital in Romford.

He was finally demobilized from the Army on 21 February 1919 having served for nearly fourteen years.

On the CWGC website there is nobody with the surname of Graygoose, however there is an **A. Greygoose** (12640) who was a lance corporal in the 2nd Battalion of the Essex Regiment. He was killed on 1 July 1916, the first day of the Battle of the Somme. He is buried at the Sucrerie Military Cemetery in Colinchamps, on the Somme.

Albert Greygoose is also commemorated on the Orsett war memorial where his name is spelt correctly.

Albert Charles Crow is not only recorded on the Stifford war memorial, he is also buried in the cemetery at St Mary's Church where the memorial is situated.

Albert Charles Crow (325439) was a private in the 9th Battalion the Essex Regiment and aged 21 when he died on 7 June 1918. He was badly wounded whilst serving on the Western Front and was sent back to the UK. He subsequently died of his wounds at home. His parents, John and Emily Crow lived at 25 London Road, South Stifford, Grays, Essex.

Albert's brother, **George Frederick Crow** (12553), aged 21, was a private serving with the 1st Battalion, the Coldstream Guards. He died during the Battle of Loos on 28 September 1915. He has no known grave and his name is commemorated on the Loos War Memorial in the Pas de Calais, which was unveiled on 4 August 1930.

Harold William Bransden (240563) was a lance corporal in the 1st/14th King's Own (Royal Lancaster Regiment) when he was killed on 9 April 1918. He was aged 26 and his name is also commemorated on the Loos War Memorial.

His parents, Walter and Jessie Robertson Bransden, lived at North Stifford, Grays, Essex. Harold also had an older brother, Walter Joseph Bransden, who was a teacher.

Albert John England (G/42860) was a private in the 16th Battalion of the Middlesex Regiment when he was killed aged 20, on 1 December 1917. His name is commemorated on the Cambrai War Memorial at Louverval in the Nord region of France.

His parents, John and Eliza England, lived at 'Browns Cottage', Westbrooke, North Stifford, Grays, Essex. Albert had two sisters, May (15) and Myrtle (7) and a brother, Charles, who was only two months old.

Tilbury War Memorial
The Clock Tower War Memorial is located in the civic square in Tilbury Town Centre. It's a resplendent way for so many good men to be remembered.

The names of the one hundred and fifty-five men who are commemorated on the memorial are recorded below. We will look at a few of them in more detail further on in the chapter.

Tilbury War Memorial (Stephen Wynn)

Royal Navy &
Mercantile Marine
Abbot H.J.
Finch J.E.
Finn J.
Ansell S.
Gaywood J.
Grattage S.
Barwick G.W.
Hardwicke C.
Harrison J.
Belton A.
Higgs G.W.H.
Hunter A.
Best A.
James W.
James W.G.
Butler A.
Macey V.
Martin E.
Cowley J.
Martyn E.T.
McIntyre J.
Dunn R.
Moore J.
Palmer A.
Phillips J.
Povey G.
Sandy A.C.
Slater J.
Smith J.W.
Talbot E.T.L.
Talbot E.T.S.
Taylor L.
Toomey J.
Treadwell W.
Webb A.R.
Wickford F.

Wilson A.
Witt J.
Wood F.

Military
Ansell A.E.
Ansell A.
Arnold J.G.
Asplin E.
Austin C.
Baker P.E.
Bleckwen H.
Blowers J.C.
Boosey R.
Brazier P.G.
Brown A.C.
Brown C.H.N.
Brown J.
Bruce W.A.
Burgess E.
Burningham E.
Cader C.
Caddy T.
Catchpole W.
Coley P.
Cooper W.
Cricket W.
Days H.
Denham E.
Dixon S.
Dowman C F.
East G.
Elliot N.W.
Elliot P.W.
Farrow J.J.
Ferdinand G.
Finch R.
Fordham A.G.

Freeman W.D.
Fulcher F.
Gannsford H.C.
Gentry C.
Gibson A.G.
Giggins G.H.
Gilling F.G.
Godden W.J.
Goodfellow E.
Gower W.G.
Greaves A.
Gregory B.W.
Hatch F.W.
Hawkins P.
Higgs F.
Howard P.
Humphrey T.
Innis J.F.
Jackson F.C.
Johnson T.H.
Keegan H.C.V.
Kelly M.
Kennedy A.
Knight R.
Laker R.G.
Larness W.
Laurie T.R.
Lawrence T.
Leeks A.E.
Lince C.
Luck E.W.
Mann B.
Marshall F.E.
Meridan A.
Mills F.
Mills J.
Mills M.
Morgan W.

Mustoe G.H.	Sherress E.M.	Tredwell A.
Mustoe J.	Slowley G.	Tredwell G.
Mustoe W.	Smith E.C.	Wallis R.
Newman A.V.	Sowells J.R.	Wallis S.
Oaden H.T.	Spooner A.	Webster A.G.
O'Connell D.F.	Spooner A.C.	Weeks H.G.
O'Neil W.T.	Stadden J.	Wesley J.
Palmer J.	Stanton W.	Whiffen A.
Percy E.	Stone W.H.	Witts J.C.
Pike R.M.	Taylor W.	Wright J.
Rankin A.	Taylor W.M.	Bown C.C.
Rayson F.	Terry E.	Cole C.
Rowkins R.T.	Terry W.	Ogden H.C.
Rowsell A.	Thompson F.	Turnnidge W.R.
Savill J.F.	Tibble A.	Wallis E.

Edward George Minter Sherress (19964) was a private in the 9th Battalion the Essex Regiment. He was 20 years of age when he died on 18 July 1917. His parents, John William and Sophia Sherress, lived at 145 & 146 The Dwellings, Tilbury Buildings, Tilbury, Essex. Edward is buried at the Faubourg D'Amiens Cemetery in Arras, France.

The following is taken from the historical notes of the CWGC entry for Faubourg-d'Amiens Cemetery.

'The French handed over Arras to Commonwealth forces in the spring of 1916 and the system of tunnels upon which the town is built were used and developed in preparation for the major offensive planned for April 1917.

The Commonwealth section of the cemetery was begun in March 1916 and it continued to be used by field ambulances and Commonwealth fighting units right up until November 1918.

The cemetery contains over 2,650 Commonwealth graves from the First World War, 10 of which are unidentified. The adjacent Arras Memorial commemorates almost 35,000 servicemen from the United Kingdom, South Africa and New Zealand who died in the Arras sector between the spring of 1916

Faubourg-d'Amiens Cemetery (Commonwealth War Graves Commission)

and 7 August 1918, and who have no known grave. The most conspicuous events of this period were the Arras offensive of April-May 1917, and the German attack in the spring of 1918.'

The 1911 Census shows Edgar had four brothers, John William (22), Thomas (18), Joseph (12) and George (7). He also had five sisters, Nelly (20), Sophia (14), Jennie (10), Marguerite (4) and Ann (2). Even by the standards of the day, ten children in a family was a lot, which perhaps explains why the family address covers two properties.

Enoch Goodfellow (345010) was a private in the 1st/1st Battalion of the Cambridgeshire Regiment, when he was killed on 8 August 1918. He is buried at the Beacon Cemetery, Sailly-Laurette in the Somme region of France.

Enoch's mother, Emily Lawrence, lived at number 26 Sydney Road, Tilbury Docks, Tilbury, Essex.

The 1911 Census showed Emily was married to a William Lawrence and they had a 7-year-old daughter, also named Emily. It would appear that she had been married previously, to Enoch's father. Besides Enoch, Emily had three other sons, Charles Goodfellow (22), Herbert (21), and Cecil (17). Emily also had another daughter, Lily Goodfellow (19).

Enoch's brother, **Cecil Goodfellow**, (27562) also served during the First World War. He was nearly 22 when he enlisted at Warley as a private in the 6th Battalion, the Border Regiment on 10 December 1915, prior to which he had been a labourer working at Tilbury Docks.

On 15 March 1918, Cecil, appeared before a medical board and was discharged from the army as being 'no longer physically fit for war service'. He was given £1 and a suit of plain clothes and sent home on warrant to await instructions as to his final discharge.

It is most likely that, because of their ages, Enoch's other brothers, Charles and Herbert, would have also served during the war as well. All we can say with any degree of certainty was if they did serve then they both survived. We have been unable to find any military records for them. Unfortunately forty per cent of service records for ranks other than officers who served in the First World War were destroyed during a German air raid on London in 1940.

Samuel Thomas Grattage (299157) was a leading stoker in the Royal Navy and serving on board HMS *Aboukir* at the time of his death on 22 September 1914. He is commemorated on the Chatham Naval Memorial.

HMS *Aboukir* was a Cressy class armoured cruiser of the British Royal Navy. At the start of the war, she was assigned to patrol an area of the North Sea in support of a force of destroyers and submarines that were based at Harwich on the Essex coast line. Their purpose was to protect the eastern end of the English Channel from the German Navy in their attacks on shipping travelling between England and France.

About 6am on 22 September 1914 HMS *Aboukir* was patrolling along with HMS *Bacchante, Euryalus, Hogue* and *Cressy*. During this particular patrol HMS *Bacchante* had to return to her base to refuel. On board her that day was Rear Admiral Arthur Christian.

Unbeknown to the three remaining ships, including HMS *Aboukir*, they had been spotted by the German submarine, *U-9* which was commanded by Kapitänleutnant Otto Weddigen. *U-9* managed to remain undetected by any of the three British cruisers. Weddigen closed in before firing a single torpedo which struck HMS *Aboukir* breaking her back. She sank within twenty minutes taking 527 of her crew to a watery grave.

In the confusion which followed HMS *Cressy* and *Hogue* were unaware that their sister ship had been attacked by a German U-boat, believing instead that she had struck a floating mine. Both ships sped to the aid of the stricken vessel in the hope of picking up any survivors. Weddigen and his *U-9* submarine, which had not yet been detected, fired two more torpedoes into HMS *Hogue* sinking her as well. The captain of HMS *Cressy*, now realising they were under attack, tried to make good his escape, but before he could do so, Weddigen fired two more torpedoes sinking HMS *Cressy* and sending her to the bottom of the sea.

In less than two hours the British Navy had lost three of its warships and the lives of 62 officers and 1,397 ratings. Samuel Grattage was one of them.

Edgar Charles Burningham (S/8902) was only just 18 when he enlisted at Gravesend in Kent and became a private in the 1st Battalion, the Queen's Own (Royal West Kent Regiment) when he was killed on 5 May 1915. He has no known grave and his name is commemorated on the Ypres Menin Gate Memorial.

At the time of the 1911 Census Edgar's family are shown as living at 13 Terront Road, West Green Road, South Tottenham, London. His parents, Edgar and Clara, had two other children besides Edgar, Reginald (10), and Winifred (18).

We have found no obvious connection between Edgar and Tilbury, so we can only assume that he moved to the area after the 1911 Census had been carried out.

Albert Edward Ansell (14834) was a private in 'A' Company, 10th Battalion, The Essex Regiment when he was killed on 24 March 1918. He was 29 years of age at the time of his death and has no known grave. He is commemorated on the Pozières War Memorial on the Somme.

His parents, William and Catherine Ansell, lived at 5 Sydney Road, Tilbury, Essex. The 1911 Census shows that besides Albert, they had eight other children, including four sons: Alfred William (23), Percy (18), David Thomas (13), Ernest Leonard (10) and three daughters, Rose Elizabeth (26), Catherine Maud (20), and Doris Evelyn (8).

We therefore already know that 'Ansell S', who is also shown on the Tilbury War memorial, is not a brother of Albert Edward Ansell. It is quite possible that they were cousins.

We believe this to be **Sydney Hubert Ansell** (1043) who was a private in the 2nd Battalion of the East Surrey Regiment when he was killed, aged 26, on 25 April 1915. He is commemorated on the Menin Gate Memorial at Ypres.

The CWGC website shows his parents as Charles M. (deceased) and Amelia Ansell, of 24 Whitehall Road, Grays, Essex. The 1911 Census shows the family home as 13 Chadwell Road, Little Thurrock, Grays, Essex. Prior to enlisting, Sydney, was a railway clerk.

The Tilbury War Memorial shows a third 'Ansell' in the shape of Ansell A. There are numerous individuals with the same details on both the CWGC website and the 1911 Census, but nobody who we feel able to confirm as being the same person with any degree of certainty.

Ernest Thomas Sillick Talbot (SS/102740), was a stoker 1st Class in the Royal Navy and a crew member of HMS *Mimosa*, when he died aged 33 on 1 June 1919. He passed away in the Royal Naval Hospital in Malta. In his will Ernest left his wife Florence £257, a large sum of money in those days.

His parents, Frank and Susan Talbot, lived in Devonport, but his wife, Florence Ada Talbot, lived at number 32 Montreal Road, Tilbury, Essex. Ernest is buried in the Malta (Capuccini) Naval Cemetery.

Alfred Tibble (147912) was an acting second corporal in the 253rd Tunnelling Company, Corps of the Royal Engineers when he was killed on 6 August 1917. He had formerly been a private (6692) in the Middlesex Regiment.

He enlisted at nearby Grays and is buried at the Bleuet Farm Cemetery in West Flanders. The Farm was used as a dressing station during 1917 Allied offensive on this front. The cemetery was begun in

Naval Cemetery in Malta. (Commonwealth War Graves Commission)

Bleuet Farm Cemetery. (Commonwealth War Graves Commission)

a corner of the farm and was in use from June to December 1917. It contains 442 graves from the First World War.

According to the 1911 Census Alfred lived at number 7 Triangle Terrace, West Thurrock, Grays, Essex. Before he enlisted in the Army he was a labourer at a local cement factory and lived with his wife, Alice, her three children from a previous marriage, twins Henry and William Gilson (9) and Violet May Gilson (5). Alfred and Alice had a son, Alfred, who was three months old.

FOR YOUR TOMORROW WE
GAVE OUR TODAY. AT
THE GOING DOWN OF THE
SUN AND IN THE MORNING
WE WILL REMEMBER THEM.

Inscription on the Memorial (Stephen Wynn)

Tilbury Port of London Authority War Memorial
The Port of London Authority (PLA) came into being on 31 March 1909 and its first major project was a deep-water shipping channel and the Tilbury Docks extension.

Within a month of the beginning of the First World War, more than 800 PLA workers had joined the armed forces and by the end of it this number had risen to 3,629. In total 403 of them were killed with another 700 injured or wounded.

Of those who enlisted 119 were awarded medals for gallantry and bravery, the names of eight of them are recorded on the 'Tablets'.

The two enormous wall plaques that make up the Port of London Authority (PLA) First World Memorial, are in the Chapel area of the

WORLD WAR I MEMORIAL TABLETS

The memorial to the members of staff of the Port of London Authority who lost their lives in the Great War (1914-18), takes the form of two marble tablets, inscribed with the names of those who fell, set into the walls of the chapel in the London International Cruise Terminal.

The memorial, designed by Sir Edwin Cooper FRIBA, the architect of the original P.L.A. Head Office building at Trinity Square, was unveiled by Admiral of the Fleet the Right Hon. Earl Beatty OM, GCB, GCVO, DSO and was dedicated by the Bishop of London, on 132 November 1952.

Within a month of the outbreak of the First World War, more than eight hundred members of staff joined the forces, and before the conclusion of hostilities, three thousand six hundred and twenty nine men had joined up. Four hundred and three of these were killed or died while serving with the colours (Navy 49; Army 345; Air Force 9). More than seven hundred were wounded or temporarily disabled through illness.

Decorations for distinguished service were awarded to no fewer than one hundred and nineteen members of staff, including two Victoria Crosses, one French Medaille Militaire, one Russian Medal of St. George, one Russian Gold Medal for Zeal, and two Italian Medals for Valour.

Memorial Tablet Notes.(Stephen Wynn)

Memorial Plaque. (Stephen Wynn)

Memorial Plaque Crest. (Stephen Wynn)

London Cruise Terminal at Tilbury Docks. The photographs were taken in the build-up to the 2013 Remembrance Day service, which the PLA put on for its staff, invited guests and local dignitaries every year on 11 November regardless of what day of the week that falls on.

The crest at the top of each plaque is that of the Port of London Authority (PLA) and is the helmet badge which is worn by the PLA Police. The Latin words, *Floreat Imperii Portus* which appear in the scroll at the bottom of the crest mean, 'Let the Imperial Port Flourish'.

Immediately underneath the crest are the Latin words, *Ad Majorem Dei gloriam*. The words translate 'For the greater glory of God' and is the Latin motto of the Society of Jesus, a religious order within the auspices of the Catholic Church who are better known by their informal name, that of Jesuits.

The above plaque also adorns one of the walls in the chapel at the London Cruise Terminal at Tilbury Docks, which is slightly confusing.

Originally the two First World War Memorial Plaques were situated at the PLA Head Offices in Trinity Square in the City of London.

According to records held by the Imperial War Museum, the initial unveiling ceremony of these plaques took place on 28 January 1926 and was carried out by the First Sea Lord Earl Beatty. The dedication was given by the Bishop of London.

The tablets were re-dedicated at their current location at Tilbury on 19 November 1990 by the Bishop of Bradwell. The tablets were then moved to their current location in 1971 after the offices where they originally stood in London were sold.

As was mentioned earlier eight of the men who were awarded medals for gallantry and bravery are recorded on the tablets. They are:

Alfred George Drake VC (S/107) was a corporal in the 8th Battalion, The Rifle Brigade and was only 22 years of age when he was killed in action on 23 November 1915, near La Brique in Belgium. For his actions, that day he was posthumously awarded the Victoria Cross. He was buried at the military cemetery in La Brique. His parents, Robert and Mary Ann Drake, lived at 62 Copley Street, Stepney, London.

The following is an extract taken from *The London Gazette* dated 21 January 1916 and is the citation for the award of his Victoria Cross.

'For most conspicuous bravery on the night of 23rd Nov., 1915, near La Brique, Belgium. He was one of a patrol of four which was reconnoitring towards the German lines. The patrol was discovered when close to the enemy who opened heavy fire with rifles and a machine gun, wounding the officer and one man. The latter was carried back by the last remaining man. Corporal Drake remained with his officer and was last seen kneeling beside him and bandaging his wounds regardless of the enemy's fire. Later a rescue party crawling near the German lines found the officer and Corporal, the former unconscious but alive and bandaged, Corporal Drake beside him dead and riddled with bullets. He had given his own life and saved his officer.'

James Burns DSC (Distinguished Service Cross) was a lieutenant in the Royal Navy Reserve when killed on 21 August 1917 when the ship he was serving on, HMS *Vala*, sank when it was hit by two torpedoes fired from German Submarine, *UB-54*. Forty-three members of the crew lost their lives. She was sailing out of Milford Haven with orders to cruise between the Fastnet and the Scilly Isles; she was never seen or heard of again. On 7 September 1917 the German government announced that HMS *Vala* had been sunk by one of their U-boats. HMS *Vala* had been involved in eight other incidents involving German U-boats in a nine-month period prior to her sinking. The vessel was a Q-ship, which was also referred to as a decoy vessel. They were heavily armed merchant ships with concealed weaponry. The Q-ships were designed to lure German submarines into making surface attacks.

Edward Allen Roe MC was a captain in the East Surrey Regiment and was attached to the 2nd/4th Battalion, Queen's Royal Regiment (West Surrey) when he was killed on 2 September 1918, aged 23. He was buried at the Reninghelst New Military Cemetery near Ypres.

His parents, Frederick Edward and Lucy Isobel Roe, lived at 'The Ridgeway' 58 Canterbury Grove, West Norwood, London.

W.J. May MC was a second lieutenant in the 2nd Battalion of the West Yorkshire Regiment (Prince of Wales's Own). He was killed on 1 August 1917. He is buried at the Lijssenthoek Military Cemetery in the West Flanders region of Belgium. His parents, Clara Elizabeth and John Alchin May lived at 14 Roy Road, Northwood, Middlesex.

Hugh Geoffrey Warner MM (8011) was a corporal in the 11th Battalion of the Royal Fusiliers when he was killed on 7 August 1918, aged 27. He is commemorated on the Pozières War Memorial on the Somme.

His parents, Frederick and Clara M Warner, lived at 67, 1 Landseer Road, Bush Hill Park, Enfield, Middlesex.

Bruce Barnard MM (630967) was a sergeant. The PLA Plaque shows him as being in the Royal Fusiliers whilst the CWGC website shows him as being in the 1st/20th Battalion of the London Regiment. He is the only one of that name on the CWGC website and on both the website and the plaque he is shown as a sergeant who has won the Military Medal.

Aged 25, he was killed on 1 September 1918 and is commemorated on the Vis-en-Artois War Memorial in the Pas-de-Calais which bears

the names of some 9,000 men who fell in the period from 8 August –
11 November 1918 in the advance to victory in Picardy and Artois, and
who have no known grave.

His parents, Mr and Mrs Robert Barnard, lived at 62 Cressingham
Road, Lewisham, London.

Arthur Moran MM (27824) was a bombardier in the 34th Trench
Mortar Battery of the Royal Garrison Artillery. He was killed on 6
February 1917. He was 29 years of age and is buried at the Cite
Bonjean Military Cemetery in Armentières in the Nord region of
France.

His parents, William and Hannah Moran, lived in Eynesbury, St
Neots in Huntingdonshire. His wife, Amelia May Moran, lived at 31
Morrison Buildings, South Commercial Road, London.

E.G. Palfrey MM (12827) was a corporal in the 1st Battalion
Grenadier Guards when he was killed on 5 April 1918, aged 29. He is
buried in the Gezaincourt Communal Cemetery extension. His parents,
Charles and Emily Palfrey, lived in Pershore, Worcestershire.

Even though none of those commemorated on the PLA plaques are
from the Thurrock area we still thought it right to include this memorial
in the book, however we have not to recorded all of their names.

CHAPTER 27

Church Plaques

There are at least seven churches across the district of Thurrock which have their own individual memorial plaques or rolls of honour commemorating the lives of men from their parishes who were killed during the First World War. Most of these names are also included on the numerous war memorials included in this book.

You will notice the numerous different ways in which each town or village chose to record the names of its fallen heroes. Some start with the man's surname followed by his initials whilst others record the same in reverse. Some include the man's full name whilst others include rank and the regiment to which they belonged.

The plaque in **Corringham Church** has twelve names on it.

C. Bragg.	W. Hamil.	W.F. Jiggins
F.W. Knowles.	J.F. Knowles.	G. Spooner.
R. Hamil.	E.J. Hollingbread	T. King
H.E. Knowles.	C. Robinson.	J. Young.

The following inscription is also included on the plaque.

'Glory to God

In Loving Memory of
The Corringham Men
Who gave their lives
For King and Country

In The
Great War 1914 – 1918
Live Thou for England
We died for England'

James Frederick Knowles, Herbert Edward Knowles and Francis William Knowles were brothers.

James Frederick Knowles (119678) was a private in the Royal Garrison Artillery before transferring to the 906th Company Labour Corps. He was 25 years of age when he was killed on 30 March 1918. He is commemorated on the Pozières War Memorial, on the Somme.

On the 1911 Census he is shown as living at Near Forge, Corringham, Essex. His parents were William and Mary Ann Knowles. He had five brothers and three sisters. James was single and shown as being a farm worker.

Francis William Knowles (26740) was a private in the 10th Battalion, the Essex Regiment when he was killed on 20 July 1916 in Flanders. He enlisted at Thames Haven in Essex and is commemorated on the Thiepval War Memorial on the Somme.

Herbert Edward Knowles was a 13-year-old schoolboy in 1911, so at the outbreak of the war he was still only 16 years of age. By the time he became another of the war's victims and the second of the Knowles family to be killed, he was only 19.

He was a corporal in the 235th Brigade of the Royal Field Artillery when he was killed on 31 May 1917. He is buried at the very British-sounding cemetery, Bedford House, in Ypres.

The cemetery became known as Bedford House after British troops renamed the nearby Chateau Rosendal, a large country house, with the same name.

Of the other three brothers, two of them, George Henry Knowles and Arthur Ernest Knowles were also old enough to have served during the First World War. The 1911 Census shows George as being 24 years of age and Arthur as being 15. Although it is almost inconceivable to believe that neither George nor Arthur served during the war, a search on Ancestry.co.uk, has not brought up any direct match. The medal roll index cards for the First World War show a possible nine matches for a George Henry Knowles, but that's as close as we can get. The same lists show one direct match for an Arthur Ernest Knowles who was in a private in both the Bedfordshire Regiment (52138) and the Norfolk Regiment (39204). There are another three A. Knowles shown as well as a further sixty Arthur Knowles.

A plaque in **St Clement's Church** in West Thurrock that has the names of sixty-seven men engraved on it. The inscription reads.

'Sacred to the memory of the brave men who died for YOU in the Great War 1914 – 1919.'

St Clements Church Plaque. (Stephen Wynn)

Lt. Branden W.G.
Pvt. Bearman F.
Pvt. Lighten S.
Pvt. Barton L.
Pvt. Lighten A.
Pvt. Brown J.J.
Cpl. Mann H.B. (MM)
Pvt. Kirby J.
Pvt. Knight F.
Pvt. Lloyd E
Pvt. Lloyd A
Pvt. Coote G
Pvt. Chapman E A
Pvt. Clark E
Pvt. Cook R
Sgt. Fogg C
Drv. Faulkner W
Pvt. French W.H.
Sgt. Galley F.T.
L/Cpl. Greatrex L.A.
Pvt. Gilbey G.H.
Pvt. Gilman H.
Pvt. Howard H.
Pvt. Howarth F.J.E.
Pvt. May A.G.
Pvt. May L.
Pvt. Monk C.E.
Pvt. Mynot H.
Pvt. Martin W.
L/Cpl. North A.
Pvt. Nash J.

Pvt. Orton J.
Cpl. Parker C.P.
L/Cpl. Parmenter A.E.
Pvt. Potter S.D.
Pvt. Padgham J.
Pvt. Patient J.
Cpl. Steward D.J.
Tr. Steward C.W.
Pvt. Steward G.E.
Br. Sparrowham E.G.
Pvt. Saunders J.W.
Pvt. Steel A.
Pvt. Stokes E.W.
Pvt. Sharp R
Pvt. Soloman H.H.
Pvt. Suttling E.E.
Cpl. Tibble A.
Br. Turner A.
Pvt. Thurley W.R.
Pvt. Thorne J.R.
Pvt. Thurgood J.H.
Cpl. Vaughan H.J.
Pvt. Vaughan G.
L/Cpl. Valentine W.J.
Pvt. Vinton H.R.
Pvt. Vaughan P.
Drv. Whiting W.A.J.
Pvt. Wright A.L.
Pvt. Wood G.
Pvt. Webb A.G.

Harold MANN MM (12669) (Military Medal) was a corporal in the 9th Battalion, the Essex Regiment, when he was killed on 8 July 1916, a week in to the Battle of the Somme. He is commemorated on the Thiepval War Memorial on the Somme.

The 9th Battalion of the Essex Regiment was formed in August 1914 at Warley near Brentwood in Essex, in August 1912. It was a service battalion and was part of 35 Brigade in the 12th Division of the British Army. Soon after its formation it moved to Shorncliffe Barracks and in March 1915 it moved again, this time to Blenheim Barracks in Aldershot. On 31 May 1915 the 9th Battalion landed at Boulogne in France. (1914-1918.net/essex.htm)

Percy Vaughan was a private (201267) in the 4th Battalion, the Essex Regiment when he was killed on 2 October 1917, aged 25. His parents, William and Alice M. Vaughan, lived at 20 Flint Street, West Thurrock, Grays.

He is commemorated on the Jerusalem Memorial which stands in the Jerusalem War Cemetery which is about 2 miles north of the historic walled city at the north end of the Mount of Olives and to the west of Mount Scopus. There is an Australian War Memorial opposite the cemetery entrance.

At the outbreak of the First World War, Palestine, which is now Israel, was then part

Jerusalem War Cemetery and plaque.
(Commonwealth War Graves Commission)

of the Ottoman Empire and was a Turkish stronghold. It was eventually entered by Allied forces in December 1916. The advance on to Jerusalem took another year, but between the start of the war in August 1914 until December 1917, some 250 Commonwealth prisoners of war, were buried in the German and Anglo-German cemeteries which are situated around the city.

Albert George May (SS/7312) was a private in the Army Service Corps when he was killed on 17 May 1918, aged 43. He must have died of wounds in the UK as he is buried in Reading Cemetery. He was survived by his widow, Maude E. May of 245 Kingston Road, New Malden, Surrey.

Reading Cemetery. (Commonwealth War Graves Commission)

Leonard May (16290) was a private in the 1st Battalion the Essex Regiment when he was killed on 28 June 1916, whilst involved in heavy fighting at Gallipoli. Prior to enlisting in the Army he had been a cement worker at one of the numerous quarries which existed in the Grays area at the time. His name is commemorated on the Helles War Memorial in Turkey. His parents, John Thomas and Kate May lived at Home Farm, London Road, West Thurrock in Grays.

Leonard had six younger sisters and a brother, Edward May, who was 18 years of age in the 1911 census.

Samuel Lighten (G/63285) lived at 6 Palmerston Cottages, West Thurrock, Grays, with his parents, Arthur and Mary-Ann Lighten. With five elder brothers and three elder sisters to contend with, Samuel was the baby of the family, so when he was killed in action on 1 September 1918 he must have had lots of people grieving for him.

When he enlisted at Grays on 15 August 1915 he was aged 25, but at 5 feet 6 inches tall and only just over 9 stone in weight, he wasn't physically a big man by today's standards.

Samuel landed at Boulogne on 31 March 1918 as a member of the 13th Battalion, the Essex Regiment. The next day he was transferred to the 12th Battalion the Suffolk Regiment, before moving on to the Middlesex Regiment ending up with the 19th Battalion, the London Regiment. He is remembered on the Vis-en-Artois Memorial.

A. Lighten would appear to be **Alfred Lighten** (6757) who is shown on the 1911 Census as living at 26 Flint Street, West Thurrock, Grays, Essex. Alfred had two younger brothers, Frederick (16) and Charles (12). Although not Samuel Lighten's brother, we would suggest he and Alfred were related to one another, especially as their addresses at Flint Street and Palmerston Cottages were not far apart.

Alfred was a sapper in the 15th Field Company of the Australian Engineers when he was killed whilst serving in France on 4 August 1916. He was 27 years of age and is buried at the Anzac Cemetery, in Sailly-sur-la-Lys, in the Pas-de-Calais region of France.

Alfred Lighten lived only three doors away from Percy Vaughan, mentioned previously, which would strongly suggest that the two men knew each other, highlighting just how closely connected communities were during the First World War.

Henry Joseph Vaughan (26286) was a corporal in the 9th Battalion, the Essex Regiment when he was killed in action on 17 July 1917. He is commemorated on the Arras War Memorial. Aged 36 at the time of his death, he was older than most soldiers.

He was the son of Samuel and Julia E. Vaughan of 2 Dalhia Terrace, West Tilbury, Grays, Essex.

George Vaughan (27258) was a private in the 1st Battalion, the Essex Regiment when he was killed on 30 November 1917 whilst serving in

Arras Cemetery. (Commonwealth War Graves Comission)

France. He is commemorated on the Cambrai Memorial within the Louverval military cemetery, France.

The memorial commemorates more than 7,000 servicemen from the United Kingdom and South Africa who were killed at the Battle of Cambrai between November and December 1917 and who have no known grave.

The Commonwealth War Graves Commission provides an excellent description of the War Memorial at Cambrai and the fighting which, in the main, was the cause of those who are commemorated there.

Sir Douglas Haig described the Cambrai operation as the gaining of a 'local success by a sudden attack at a point where the enemy did not expect it'. To some extent he succeeded in his objective.

The method of assault which Haig used was new. For the first time there was no warning to the Germans of an imminent infantry attack by preceding it with a preliminary artillery bombardment. Instead he

Cambrai War Memorial. (Commonwealth War Graves Commission)

chose to use tanks to try and break through the German lines, with his infantry following up behind with the added protection of the cover of smoke.

The attack, which began early in the morning of 20 November 1917, must have been somewhat confusing for the Germans. It can only be assumed that they must have been taken by surprise and were not expecting to see infantry soldiers following up behind the tanks.

Initially the attack was a success, but by 22 November, Haig decided to call a halt so allowing his men to be able to rest and reorganise themselves. There will always be discussion and disagreement amongst historians and military experts as to whether tactically that was the right decision for Haig to have made, but one fact is undeniable, this move allowed the Germans to reinforce their defences.

Between 23 to 28 November, with the offensive having resumed, the fighting concentrated almost entirely around the area of Bourlon Wood. By 29 November, it had become clear that the enemy were ready to launch a major counter-attack.

Over the next five days the fighting was intense, with much of the ground which Haig had gained during the initial days of the attack, being lost. Despite the early successes for the Allies, the overall gains were ultimately disappointing but they had learnt a new military tactic with the use of the tanks as their main weapon.

George's mother, Alice Vaughan, lived at 8 St Georges Terrace, West Thurrock, Grays and, according to the 1911 Census, she had two other sons, Arthur Edward Vaughan (33) and Walter Vaughan (23).

The story of the four Steward brothers who fought in the First World War is a truly remarkable one. David James Steward, George Edward Steward and Charles William Steward, were all killed, whilst William Henry Steward, although being wounded three times, against all the odds survived and returned home.

Charles William Steward (81194) was the first of the brothers to die when he was killed on 11 April 1917. He was a private in the Essex Yeomanry who were involved in the spring offensive against the Germans which took place along the Arras front, and began in April 1917.

At the time of his death he was 26 years of age. His parents, James William and Elizabeth Mary Steward, lived at 9 Tunnel Cottage, West Thurrock, Grays, Essex.

George Edward Steward (99224) was the second brother to be killed when he fell on 6 April 1918, just a matter of days before the first anniversary of Charles's death. Aged 20, George was a private in the 37th Battalion of the Machine Gun Corps. He is buried in Gezaincourt Communal Cemetery on the Somme.

David James Steward (23651) was the last of the brothers to die on 25 June 1918. He was a lance corporal with the 13th Battalion, the Essex Regiment. The interesting point here is that although David was from Grays, the 13th Battalion was also the West Ham Pals Regiment, it was a Service regiment and had been raised in the Borough of West Ham by the then Mayor, Councillor Crow, on 27 December 1914. It moved to Brentwood in May 1915, one would assume to the barracks at Warley, which was the home of the Essex Regiment.

The entire regiment, some 1,200 men, landed at Boulogne in France on 17 November 1915 and was finally disbanded in February 1918, which begs the question how it is recorded that David James Steward was, at the time of his death on 25 June 1918, a member of the 13th Battalion, Essex Regiment, four months after that battalion had been disbanded.

It is assumed that David died as a prisoner of war since he is buried in Niederzwehren in Germany, in a cemetery which was begun in 1915 for the burial of prisoners of war who died at the nearby camp. During the First World War there were nearly 3,000 Allied soldiers and civilians buried there.

William Henry Steward (28757) was a corporal in the 6th Battalion, 11 Company, Machine Gun Corps. He enlisted aged 24 on 14 November 1914 at Grays and was demobilized on 11 April 1919.

According to his Army service record he was injured three times during the war, twice by being gassed and once when he was shot. On 30 July 1916 he suffered gunshot wounds to the face, back and hand. Initially he was admitted to a field hospital in France before being returned to the UK on 13 August 1916. He was subsequently sent back to France, indicating that his wounds were not of a serious nature.

On 5 November 1917 he was gassed and returned to the UK on 13 November 1917 where he was admitted to the Wharncliff General Hospital in Sheffield on 16 November 1917. He once again returned to France and was gassed a second time on 9 April 1918.

When he was sent back to the UK after receiving his gunshot wounds and admitted to hospital on 13 August 1916, he was a lance corporal, his records show that whilst he was in hospital he reverted to the rank of private. He was eventually promoted to the substantive rank of corporal on 23 February 1917, soon after which he returned to France. On 16 March 1920 his medical record showed the following.

'Difficulties in breathing through nose. Pains in back of hand', it then goes on to say, 'No trouble from wounds. No trouble in chest.'

That seemed to be a somewhat contradictory statement. The same report also noted that he had previously suffered ear damage which was healing and was expected to be fine within a year. One assumes this was as a result of the sustained deafening noise of exploding shells whilst serving in France.

Prior to the war David had worked as builder's labourer for Jaggers Bros of Hill Rise, Vange, Pitsea, Essex. David married Laura Julia Cullum on 9 January 1921 at St Mary's Church in Camberwell, Surrey. At that time he was living at 127 Cobourg Road, Camberwell.

E.C. Sparrowham (56279) was a bombardier in 'A' Battery, 109 Brigade, Royal Field Artillery, when he was killed on 31 August 1916. He is buried in Bernafay Wood British Cemetery, Montauban on the Somme.

The 1911 Census shows one family by the name of Sparrowham living at 13 St George Terrace, West Thurrock, Grays, Essex with eight children ranging in age from 2 years to 24, but none of them with initials that resemble anything close to E.G. C.

Looking at the same family on the 1901 Census shows an Edward Sparrowham amongst the children listed. He is shown as being 10 years old. Clicking on his name shows an entry for 'UK, Soldiers Died in the Great War, 1914-1919' which then shows an entry for Edward George Charles Sparrowham, which confirms the details that are recorded on the CWGC website for E.G.C. Sparrowham.

John Padgham (27629) was a private in the 7th Battalion, the Border Regiment when he was killed on 23 April 1917, aged 40. Prior to enlisting in the army he was a labourer at nearby Tilbury Docks. His name is commemorated on the Arras War Memorial.

His father, also named John Padgham, was living at 'Kenilworth', South View Road, West Thurrock, Grays, Essex. John had two brothers who were both old enough to have fought during the war but we can find no trace of either of them having ever served in any of the armed forces.

St Mary Magdalene Church, in North Ockendon has twenty-two names recorded on its First World War Memorial Plaque, which commemorates the men from the parish who lost their lives during the Great War.

'These men of North Ockendon gave their lives to their country and to God.'

John William Barber. AB HMS *Ardent*
Ernest James Bell. Stoker 1st Class HMS *Queen Mary*
Frank Leonard Benton. Pvt. Canadian Army
George Herbert Cressy. Sgt. Seaforth Highlanders
George William Drake. Pvt. Labour Corps
John Thomas Drake. Cpl. Essex Regiment
Frederick Drury. Pvt. RAMC
Sir Frederick Eve. Lt. Col. RAMC
Joseph Harris. Petty Officer HMS *Royal Sovereign*
Herbert Walter Ketley. Cpl. Essex Regiment
Thomas Richard Mansfield. AB HMS *Hogue*
Charles Oddy. Pvt. Essex Regiment
Henry Pavitt. Pvt. Essex Regiment
Ernest Albert Richardson. Lt. Pioneers AJE
Mark Richardson. Steward HMS *Persia*
Charles Russell. Captain. Gurkha Rifles
Henry Branfill Russell. Lt. Essex Regiment
Charles Speller. Pvt. London Regiment
Alfred Thomas Spooner. Pvt. London Regiment
Harry Stokes. Pvt. Essex Regiment
Howard West-Thompson. Pvt. Sussex Regiment
Maurice West-Thompson. 2nd Lt. Royal Flying Corps

John Thomas Drake (3/2039), served his country and fell in the First
World War. He was a corporal in the 10th Battalion of the Essex
Regiment when he was killed on the battlefields of Flanders on 28
September 1916. He was 21 years of age and is commemorated on the
Thiepval War Memorial.

John's brother, **George William Drake** (41227) also died during
the war. According to the CWGC website, he was originally a private
in the 8th Battalion, the Yorkshire Regiment, but by the time of his
death on 23 October 1918, he had transferred to the 144th POW
(Prisoner of War) Company of the Labour Corps where he became
private 374060. He was 21 years of age at the time of his death and is
buried at Etaples Military Cemetery.

Interestingly the Ancestry.co.uk website shows George as
previously having been a private (6695) in the Durham Light Infantry
and not the Yorkshire Regiment.

Godewaersvelde British Cemetery. (Commonwealth War Graves Commission)

His parents George and Emily Drake, lived at Ivy Cottage, Clay Tye, North Ockendon, Essex. The 1911 Census shows Clay Tye as being in Great Warley, North Ockendon, which even allowing for the different parish and district boundaries of today, cannot be correct as Great Warley is on the outskirts of Brentwood and North Ockendon is closer to Romford.

Maurice West-Thompson, was a second lieutenant in 60 Squadron of the Royal Flying Corps when he was killed on 23 November 1917. He is buried at the Godewaersvelde British Cemetery in the Nord region of France which contains a total of 972 Commonwealth burials from the First World War, as well as 19 German war graves.

Although Maurice is recorded on the CWGC website, we could find no trace of him on the military section of Ancestry.co.uk website or either the 1901 or 1911 Census.

We have been unable to find the name Howard West-Thompson on

Headstone of Maurice & Howard West-Thompson. (Photograph with permission www.warmemorials.org)

Stone Memorial to Maurice & Howard West-Thompson. (Photograph with permission of www.warmemorials.org)

any UK census, dating back to 1881 and neither is he showing on the CWGC website.

So as not to be defeated by what had become somewhat of a conundrum, we scoured the internet to see if we could find anything further about the West-Thompson brothers, especially Howard, on whom we had found nothing at all. It was if he had never existed – that was until we came across the photographs on www.warmemorials online.org

We are not sure why, but Howard West-Thompson is buried at the Thetford Cemetery in Norfolk. Halfway down the cemetery on the west hand side of the grounds is the grave of **Howard West-Thompson** (TR/10/181817), who was a private in the 52nd Battalion of the Royal Sussex Regiment. He was killed whilst serving in France on 1 July 1918.

Next to Howard's grave are memorial stones for both Maurice and Howard. Mystery solved, although we are still not sure why two men who are commemorated on a church plaque in North Ockendon in Essex, are also commemorated in a cemetery in Thetford, Norfolk.

The gravestone of Howard West-Thompson is on the right of the picture, with the memorial stone of both Howard and Maurice on the left, which gives the suggestion that there had previously been either a cross or an obelisk standing on the stones.

That's not the end of the story. Further research on Maurice and Howard made their story even more confusing. A search of www.roll-of-honour.com came up with the following entries on the Eastbourne War Memorial in Sussex, highlighting once again just how difficult historical research can be when names are spelt or recorded differently.

In the first entry for Howard West Thompson, West is shown as a middle name rather than the first part of his surname.

'Private TR/10/181817, 52nd (Training) Battalion, Royal Sussex Regiment. Died at home of influenza 1 July 1918. Aged 18. Resident of 'Killarney' Summerdown Road, Old Town, Eastbourne. Born in Wandsworth and enlisted in Eastbourne. Employed in Eastbourne as a clerk at the London Provincial Bank. Buried in Thetford Cemetery, Norfolk.'

The fact that he died at home would explain why he is actually buried in the UK. If, like his brother Maurice, he had been killed whilst serving overseas, he would have been buried in a cemetery close to where he fell or commemorated on a nearby war memorial.

With Maurice West-Thompson, the name was once again recorded in such a way as to make 'West' appear to be a middle name rather than the first part of a hyphenated surname.

> *'2nd Lieutenant, Royal Flying Corps, killed in action on 23 November 1917 aged 19. Resident of 'Killarney' Summerdown Road, Old Town, Eastbourne. Brother of Howard Thompson. Grave location unknown.'*

Here we have two brothers who are somehow connected to separate locations in three different counties, Essex, Norfolk and Sussex, each one recording them on a local war memorial!

Henry Branfill Russell was a private in the 1st Battalion Essex Regiment and was killed on 11 July 1916, aged 21. At the time of his death his battalion were involved in the heavy fighting in the early days of the Battle of the Somme. Henry is buried at the Gezaincourt Communal Cemetery on the Somme.

He was the son of the unusually-named Champion Branfill Russell and Isabel Russell, who lived at 'Stubbers' in North Ockendon, Essex.

Charles Russell was Henry's uncle and the brother of his father, Champion. He was a captain in the Indian Army Reserve of Officers and attached to the 3rd Battalion, 3rd Queen Alexandra's Own Gurkha Rifles, when he died on 22 November 1917.

The historical notes on the CWGC website for the Jerusalem War Cemetery, where Charles is buried, record that by 21 November 1917 (the day before Charles was killed), the Egyptian Expeditionary Force had gained a line about 5 kilometres west of Jerusalem, but the city was deliberately spared bombardment and direct attack. Very severe fighting followed, lasting until the evening of 18 December, when the 53rd (Welsh) Division on the south and the 60th (London) and 74th (Yeomanry) Divisions on the west, had captured all the city's prepared defences. Turkish forces left Jerusalem throughout that night and in the morning of 9 December, the Mayor came to the Allied lines with the Turkish Governor's letter of surrender. Jerusalem was occupied that day and on 11 December, General Allenby formally entered the city, followed by representatives of France and Italy. Captain Charles Russell and his comrades did not die in vain.

He was married to Lillian Russell of Wayfoong, Steep, Petersfield, Hampshire.

Mark Richardson was born in 1898 which would have made him 16 years of age in 1914. He would have only been able to legally enlist in the armed forces on his eighteenth birthday in 1916.

The 1911 Census shows Mark as being 13 years of age. He had four brothers, one of whom had the somewhat unusual name of, Richardson Richardson, and although we have viewed the original census entry, which clearly shows that name, we can only assume it was recorded in error and should have in fact been Richard. He also had two sisters. His parents were Arthur and Sarah Richardson and the family lived at Clay Tye, Great Warley, North Ockendon.

A check on the CWGC website, throws up twenty-eight possible matches for the name 'Mark Richardson'. Four of these actually have the Christian name Mark and eight of them have the initial 'M', but none of them come up as a direct match.

The plaque in St Mary Magdelene Church in North Ockendon, records that Mark was a steward on HMS *Persia*, indicating that he was a member of the Royal Navy. The entry on the plaque is slightly misleading as it was in fact SS *Persia* which was not a war ship of the British Royal Navy, but an ocean going luxury passenger liner, belonging to the Peninsular & Oriental Steam Navigation Company Limited, better known today as P&O.

For more than ten years SS *Persia* had sailed between London and Bombay in India, on what was known at the time as the 'empire run'.

The ship left London en route to Bombay on 18 December 1915, with Commodore W.H.S. Hall (Royal Navy Reserve) at her helm. Part of the mystique about this fateful trip is that the Maharaja Jagatjit Singh was initially on board when the ship left London, with what was reportedly a £10 million fortune in gold and jewels. For some reason the Maharaja didn't leave with the ship when it sailed out of Marseilles on 26 December, although why he made that decision, isn't recorded.

Four days after leaving Marseilles, on 30 December and sailing some 71 miles off the coast of Crete, she was struck by a torpedo fired

SS Persia. *(Wikipedia)*

without warning, by the German submarine *U-38*. The time was 1.10pm; she sank in less than ten minutes. Of the 519 passengers and crew on board, 334 perished. Mark Ernest Richardson, aged 17, was one of those who lost his life.

Some of the more affluent members of society were on board the *Persia*, including Lord John Montagu of Beaulieu. With him was his secretary and mistress, Eleanor Thornton, who was said to have been the inspiration for the 'Spirit of Ecstasy' statuette which adorns the bonnet of Rolls Royce cars. Lord Montagu survived, whilst Eleanor sadly perished.

The *Persia* was the first passenger ship to be torpedoed without warning during the war, which went against international maritime law. What were known as Cruiser Rules allowed for the stopping and searching of merchant ships for contraband, by military vessels, but the ship could only be sunk if the passengers and crew were put in a place of safety, such as on board another ship or on land; even placing them in lifeboats in the open sea wasn't considered sufficient.

The commander of *U-38* was Captain Christian August Max Ahlmann Valentiner, more commonly referred to as Max Valentiner.

By sinking the SS *Persia* in the manner in which he did, he was also in breach of the Imperial German Navy's own restrictions on attacking passenger liners. The incident made headlines around the world and was front page news in British newspapers of the day.

A year earlier another German submarine had attacked and sunk the Cunard Line passenger ship, the RMS *Lusitania*, causing the deaths of 1,198 passengers and crew. This one act alone is credited with greatly influencing the decision by America to eventually enter the war in 1917.

Despite his actions, which were seen by the Allies as a war crime, Valentiner was never charged by them in the aftermath of hostilities. In fact he was feted by the German people, not only for his actions in sinking the SS *Persia* but because he had been responsible for the sinking of over 150 Allied ships, making him in the eyes of the German people, a real hero. He was rewarded with promotion and medals for his achievements and was recognised wherever he went.

Max Valentiner. (Wikipedia)

Valentiner served throughout the Second World War as the group commander of U-boat submarines in Kiel-Danzig, a position which he held until March 1945.

He died on 19 June 1949 at Sonderborg hospital from lung disease, which he is believed to have contracted as a result of inhaling toxic vapours from the engines of the U-boats he had served in during the First World War. A certain ironic ending, some would say.

Ernest Richardson was not immediately related to Mark Richardson. What we do know of him from the plaque in the church was that he was a lieutenant in the 2nd Pioneers of the Australian Infantry. The CWGC website shows that he was killed on 2 August 1918 and is commemorated on the Villers-Bretonneux War Memorial on the Somme.

The history notes on the same website record the following about the memorial:

'Villers-Bretonneux became famous in 1918 when the German advance on Amiens ended in the capture of the village by their tanks and infantry on 23 April. On the following day, the 4th and 5th Australian Divisions, with units of the 8th and 18th Divisions, recaptured the whole of the village and on 8 August, the 2nd and 5th Australian Divisions advanced form its eastern outskirts in the Battle of Amiens.

The memorial is the Australian National Memorial erected to commemorate all Australian soldiers who fought in France and Belgium during the First World War, to their dead, and especially to name those dead whose graves are not known.'

St Michael's Church at Fobbing has a memorial plaque which commemorates the names of six of its local parishioners who made the ultimate sacrifice and gave their lives during the First World War.

J. Brown	H. Webb	J. Quy
T. Collinson	B.P. Gilmore	F.G. Thurgood

B.P. Gilmore was **Bertram Percy Gilmore** (51591), a private in 'A' Company of the 1st/14th Battalion the London Regiment (London

Roll of Honour. (Stephen Wynn)

Scottish). He was born in Fobbing and was only 19 years of age when he was killed on 17 October 1917.

He had only arrived in Le Havre on 14 June 1917, joined his unit a month later on 14 July and four months later he was dead, a young life so cruelly expunged.

He was the son of George Frederick and Rhoda Gilmore of 5 Alstons Villas, Corringham, Stanford-Le-Hope, Essex. The 1911 Census showed that Bertram had two brothers, Frederick R.A. Gilmore (19) and Ernest George Gilmore (15). He also had two sisters, Dorothy R. Gilmore (18) and Grace Sydney Gilmore (6).

Ernest George Gilmore (15186) also served as a private during the war in the same battalion and regiment as Bertram. He was wounded twice during his service. On 27 December 1917 he received a gunshot wound to the hand and on 6 November 1918, less than a week to go until the end of the war, he was shot in the thigh.

On 19 January 1939 Ernest re-enlisted into the Royal Artillery Reserve, four months before the Second World War began.

We can find no record of Frederick Gilmore having served during the First World War, but as he was a school teacher, perhaps that was deemed to have been a protected profession which prevented him from enlisting.

F.G. Thurgood was in fact **Frederick George Thurgood** (248110). He was a private in the 2nd/2nd Battalion, the London Regiment (Royal Fusiliers) when he was killed on 24 April 1918. He was only 19 years of age and is commemorated at the Poizières War Memorial on the Somme.

His parents, Henry and Agnes Thurgood, lived at 1 Park Side, Bell Hill, Vange, Essex. Fredrick was born at nearby Langdon Hills, although on the 1911 Census, it clearly says Laindon Hills, which allowing for the standards of literacy at the time, was an easy mistake to make. He had four brothers, Alfred (1), John (17), Arthur (7), George (2) and a sister, Emily (11).

Having searched both ancestry.co.uk and the CWGC websites, we can find no direct match for either Alfred or John, indicating that neither of them were in the armed forces, even though they would have been within the right age range to have been so.

J. Quy was **Jim Quy** (K/44333) who was a Stoker 1st Class in the Royal Navy, serving on HMS *Racoon* when he was killed on 9 January 1918. He is commemorated on the Chatham Naval War Memorial in Kent.

HMS *Racoon* was a Beagle class, three-funnelled coal-burning destroyer. Amongst her armoury of different weaponry were four torpedoes.

In the early hours of 9 January 1918 under the command of Lieutenant George Napier and with ninety-one crew, she was on route to Lough Swilly to take up convoy and anti-submarine duties in the Northern Approaches. The weather conditions at the time were atrocious. She was operating in heavy seas and hampered even more by having to sail through a blizzard. As she approached the Garvan Isles, at the very top of Ireland, she struck rocks and sank. All ninety-two crew on board died. Those who might have survived the initial crash would not have survived for more than a matter of minutes in such extremely cold waters.

Headstone of Private J.E. Banks. (Stephen Wynn)

St Margaret's Church Roll of Honour. (Stephen Wynn)

St Margaret's Church, Stanford-le-Hope, contains two wall plaques from the First World War, one of which has the names of seventy-one men from Stanford-le-Hope. All of those named on the plaque are also named on the town's war memorial which is situated just outside the church's front gates, on a small island in the middle of the road.

One of the names on the plaque is that of Banks J.E. In the cemetery at the rear of St Margaret's Church is a Commonwealth War Graves Commission headstone in the name of **Private J.E. Banks**, (866) Essex Yeomanry, who died 30 May 1917, aged 23.

The CWGC website shows a James Edmund Banks of the 3rd/1st Essex Yeomanry. His mother, Winifred Emily Banks was living at 118 Woodfield Road, Leigh-on-Sea, Essex. Interestingly it also shows his father as 'the late' James Bank. Both father and son are buried together at St Margaret's Church at Stanford-le-Hope which shows James Banks senior died on 22 September 1922, aged 55. This shows that the information for Private Banks which is included on the CWGC entry had to have been compiled after September 1922.

Also buried at St Margaret's are the following soldiers who were killed in the First World War, but whose graves are not marked by a Commonwealth War Graves Commission headstone. They are.

F. Jackson (M/427213) was a private in the Army Service Corps, based at the MT Depot at Sydenham. He was 27 years of age when he died on 17 November 1918, six days after the Armistice. He was the son of Edward and Annie Jackson and the husband of Christina Jackson of 11 Southey Walk, Tilbury, Essex.

Patrick Lowry (T2/SR/01280) was a staff sergeant major in the 312th Company, Army Service Corps and was 55 years of age when he died 31 May 1916. Born in County Carlow, Ireland, he was married to Annie Lowry of 259 Millbrook Road, Southampton, Hampshire.

The 1911 Census shows that at the time Patrick, his wife, Annie, and their children, Ernest Patrick Lowry (23), who was born in the United Provinces in India and Florence Celia Lowry (14), who was born at Fort William, in Culcutta, were living at 'Avondale', Branksome Avenue in Stanford-le-Hope, which would explain why he was buried in St Margaret's church cemetery. Sometime between then and after the end of the First World War, Annie and the children had moved on to a new life in Southampton.

Ancestry.co.uk shows that Patrick had previously been in the army in the Indian Supply and Transport Corps and retired in 1905 aged 45. He attested at Gravesend in Kent on 5 October 1914, and joined his regiment at Aldershot ten days later, already in the rank of staff sergeant major, one would imagine because of his mature years and his previous military service. He appeared to have been deployed in a training capacity within the United Kingdom. On 18 May 1916 he was subsequently discharged because he was 'no longer physically fit for war service' having served for a year and 201 days. It would appear that the reason for his discharge was an aggravated hernia, although he had also lost a stone in weight since he had enlisted, had thickening of the arteries and was experiencing paralysis in his right foot. Less than two weeks after his discharge he was dead.

Sadly his son **Ernest Lowry** (2043) was also a victim of the war.

He was a corporal in the 3rd (City of London) Battalion (Royal Fusiliers), London Regiment, when he was killed on the Western Front on 10 March 1915.

Both Patrick and Ernest are recorded on the roll of honour inside St Margaret's church and on the Stanford-le-Hope war memorial, but their surname on both is spelt incorrectly as 'Loury' and not Lowry.

W.J. Mead has already been mentioned in this book in the section about the war memorial at Horndon-on-the-Hill, which is situated at the town's St Peter's and Paul's church. He died on 24 August 1818 and was a sapper in the Royal Engineers.

We have not been able to establish why he has been commemorated on Horndon-on-the-Hills war memorial, yet buried at St Margaret's church in Stanford-le-Hope.

George Weald (59763) was a gunner in 'Y' Company, 23rd Trench Mortar Battery, Royal Field Artillery when he died on 2 November 1916 aged 24. He had originally enlisted at Gravesend in Kent on 19 October 1909 when he was only 18 years of age, signing on for three years which he completed on 18 October 1912, at which time he returned to 'civvy street' and a place on the Army Reserve. He was later recalled to the colours at the outbreak of the war.

George Weald Headstone.
(Stephen Wynn)

He was the son of John and Sarah Weald of Great Ganlands, Stanford-Le-Hope.

Ancestry.co.uk record the fact that the location of his death was 'at sea'. As he is buried in the cemetery at St Margaret's Church, it can only be assumed that he was wounded whilst fighting in France and died whilst at sea on route back to England.

Alfred H. Willis (330795) was a private in the Cambridgeshire and Suffolk Reserve Battalion of the Suffolk Regiment when he died on 18 November 1918, aged 18, ironically not in France or Belgium but at home, which at the time is believed to have been at Hastings in East

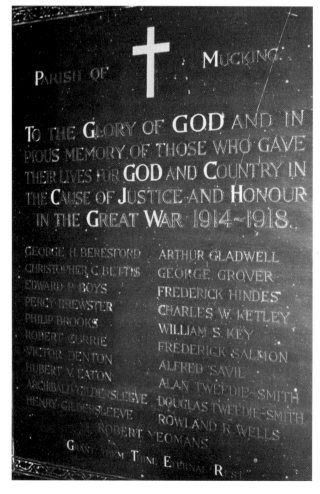

Headstone of Private Alfred Willis. (Stephen Wynn)

Mucking Church Roll of Honour. (Stephen Wynn)

Sussex. He was born in Bowers Gifford and enlisted at Warley near Brentwood.

The 1911 Census shows his family living at Mucking Heath, near Orsett. Alfred's parents were Fred and Isabella Willis, and he had three younger brothers, Leonard (7), Arthur (6) and Albert, who was only six months old.

The other plaque that can be found inside the church is the one which used to be in St John the Baptist Church in nearby Mucking until it closed in 1992.

Alan Morton Tweedie-Smith was a second lieutenant in the 1st Battalion, the Queen's (Royal West Surrey) Regiment when he was killed on 13 October 1915. He was 21 years of age and is commemorated on the Loos War Memorial.

The CWGC website shows his parents, Robert and Harriet Tweedie-Smith, as living at 'Normanhurst', The Cliffs, Westcliff-on-Sea, Essex. The 1911 Census shows Alan as a 17-year-old solicitor's articled clerk and the family as living at 4 Rayners Road, Putney, London. Alan is shown as having two sisters, Phyllis (11) and Joyce (8) and a brother, John (3). There is no sign of Douglas Tweedie-Smith on the family list.

On the 1901 Census the family is also living at number 4 Rayners Road, Putney, London. Alan is the oldest of the children, then Douglas and Leslie, who are both aged 4, one would imagine twin boys, and Phyllis who is shown as being one year old.

On the 1911 Census Douglas Tweedie-Smith is shown as being a pupil at Palmers School in Grays, Essex, which at the time was a boarding school and on the day the census was taken, he was at school in Grays rather than being at home in London.

Douglas Tweedie-Smith, as his surname is spelt on the England & Wales Death Index for the period 1916-2007, was born on 24 September 1896 in London and was educated at Palmers College in Grays, Essex, which in 1911 was a boarding school. During his early teenage years, like a lot of boys of his age, he had taken an active part in military based organisations, being part of both the Public Schools Cadet Corps as well as the London University Officer Training Corps before the war. He received a commission and joined the 15th Battalion of the Middlesex Regiment at the start of the war and in 1915 transferred to the Royal Flying Corps as a lieutenant, obtaining his pilot's certificate as well as his wings at the Military School at Shoreham on 13 July 1915, flying a Maurice Farman Biplane.

According to an article in *Flight* magazine from 1916, where his surname is shown as Tweedy-Smith, he was promoted to the position of inspector of aeroplanes at the Royal Flying Corps headquarters at Farnborough in October 1915, whilst still only 19 years of age. On 27 November 1915, while flying to France, he was delayed by snow and gales and, arriving at HQ after dark, had to descend without flares and met with a serious accident from which it took him four months to fully recover. Having returned to his duties he had to take a draft of men to France, but owing to a German submarine threat his return journey was a potentially perilous one. When he arrived back in England at Southampton he became extremely ill and was conveyed to the nearby Netley Military Hospital where he was treated. He died on 10 April 1916 at Netley Hospital.

His will shows that he left the sum of £489 4s 5d to Robert Tweedy-Smith and that his home address was 'Normanhurst' The Cliffs, Westcliff-on-Sea, Essex.

CHAPTER 28

Tilbury Fort

The River Thames has played its part in the history of England many times over the years, leading as it does to the country's capital. Before the invention of airships or aircraft the only way for an invading nation to reach the shores of Britain was by sea, and what better place to head for than London. Here is where the monarch lived, where government sat and the country's wealth was stored. With this in mind it made

The Fort's Chapel (Stephen Wynn)

White Gate. Main entrance to the Fort. (Stephen Wynn)

perfect sense that the river which runs directly to all of these prizes was well protected.

When looked at on a map of London, it is clear to see the path of the River Thames as it meanders its way from the sea and passes between Kent and Essex. As it reaches East Tilbury it turns sharply to its right and by the time it passes between Tilbury and Gravesend the river is at its narrowest point.

Tilbury Fort as it is today is still mainly the work of its designer, Sir Bernard de Gomme, who was King Charles II's chief engineer. The changes he made to the structure which was already in place, came about largely because of the 1667 debacle, when a group of Dutch naval ships sailed unchallenged up the River Thames on route to London.

The additional works had turned the old blockhouse into a formidable defensive structure. Living accommodation for both officers and other ranks was added along with gunpowder magazines and a parade square. To further add to its effectiveness, extensive gun batteries were added along the riverbanks to deal with any sea-bound attack that was heading along the Thames towards London.

Further work was carried out during the 1870s. This included additional gun batteries to the south-east, south-west and north-east bastions.

Prior to the start of the Great War in 1914 it was used as a mobilisation store, specifically for the 4th and 5th Divisional Horse Artillery, and for the storage of both large shells and smaller munitions.

The first thing that strikes a visitor to the Fort is its imposing position looking out over the river. Approaching the entrance for the paying public, one walks through the impressive Water Gate which was originally only for the passage of officers and special dignitaries. Other ranks and deliveries had to enter and leave via the Landport Gate which is situated on the north side of the Fort.

The White Gate, which was carved out of Portland stone, was designed to both impress visitors, as well as to commemorate the original building of it by Sir Bernard de Gomme. The name of Charles II is also inscribed on it, sitting immediately underneath a niche, which suggests that a statue, possibly of the king himself, had once been there, as above that is the royal coat of arms.

Above the Water Gate entrance passage is what used to be the

Water Gate entrance. (Stephen Wynn)

accommodation for the master gunner who was in charge of the Fort's artillery. Slightly to the left of that was the guard house, which is now the main reception area, a shop and a café. Above that is a chapel.

To the right of the Water Gate is a set of large double gates which were put in during the First World War after a gap was cut in the Fort's outer wall, presumably for an extra access point to deal with all the additional comings and goings of both men and equipment.

Sentry duty was carried out around the clock by a section of twelve men who were overseen by a sergeant. They were armed and would challenge everybody who wanted to enter or leave the Fort.

There are numerous old artillery pieces, now no more than museum artefacts, set out in and around the central area which was once the parade square. The two buildings which housed the gunpowder magazines, as well as the officer's quarters were still there, but the soldiers' barracks block, which was on the opposite side of the parade ground to the officer's quarters, was demolished in 1951 following bomb damage from German aircraft during the Second World War.

At the outbreak of the First World War the Fort became a barracks for troops who were waiting to be deployed to the Western Front, but in October 1915 it was officially designated as an Ordnance Depot, once again resuming its function of looking after and supplying military equipment. This included explosives, ammunition, gun carriages and wagons, all of which was looked after by men from the Army Ordnance Department.

With the commencement of German Zeppelin raids over the south coast of Britain in January 1915, anti-aircraft guns along with searchlights to deal with night raids, were installed at the Fort. The anti-aircraft batteries at Tilbury Fort saw action during a Zeppelin raid on the night of the 2/3 September 1916, which also saw the Kent ports of Chatham and Gravesend being targeted as well.

The Fort became a major British location for the storing and distribution of munitions for the war effort. For the duration of the war Captain A.A.J. Hall, along with a staff sergeant, a lance corporal and fifty soldiers were all living and working within the confines of the Fort.

Later in the war bigger and better anti-aircraft guns were added to the defences in the area, with one of the guns becoming affectionately known as 'Screaming Lizzie'. They could fire at a rate of twenty rounds per minute, which was a totally new concept and an excellent advantage for the defending British forces to have at their disposal.

After the war in June 1919, Captain Hall wrote a short history of Tilbury Fort and about his time spent there during the war.

Its military life came to an end in 1950 when it became an historic monument. Renovation of the Fort took place throughout the 1970s and it was eventually opened to the public in 1982. A year later it became one of the many properties which are now looked after and maintained by the English Heritage.

Tilbury Fort still stands today, not only as a continuous reminder of a once victorious nation from a bygone era, but also as one of the finest examples of 17th century fortifications in the country.

CHAPTER 29

Coalhouse Fort, East Tilbury

There have been fortifications at the site of Coalhouse Fort as far back as the early 1400s when earthworks were put in place to protect the village of East Tilbury from the potential threat of a French invasion.

In 1540, during the reign of King Henry VIII, a blockhouse, armed with fifteen cannon was built at the Coalhouse Fort site as part of an improvement scheme of coastal defences. Similar defences were built all along the Thames on both sides of the river to defend London.

Throughout the centuries Britain and France had always been at loggerheads with each other, rarely was there a time when the relationship between the two countries could be described as being cordial. This led to a growing mistrust and an almost constant belief on the part of British politicians as well as the monarchy, that the French might be about to invade.

In the mid 1800s ship building changed forever with the birth of ironclad ships. No longer was wood and sail in charge of the high seas, it was now the turn of iron and steam to rule the waves. This only led to further mistrust and concerns by the British that the French might once again think of invading. This led to a complete re-appraisal of coastal defences along the south coast. Out of this came the building of the Coalhouse Fort of today which was built and completed between 1861 and 1874 to help defend London from a potential attack or invasion via the River Thames, making it one of the most powerful

Route of old Railway Line. (Stephen Wynn)

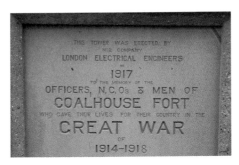

THIS TOWER WAS ERECTED BY
No2 COMPANY
LONDON ELECTRICAL ENGINEERS
IN
1917
TO THE MEMORY OF THE
OFFICERS, N.C.Os & MEN OF
COALHOUSE FORT
WHO GAVE THEIR LIVES FOR THEIR COUNTRY IN THE
GREAT WAR
OF
1914-1918

Memorial at St Catherine's Church. (Stephen Wynn)

coastal forts and the finest examples of military architecture of the Victorian era.

In 1903 the previous earthwork mounts at the nearby East Tilbury Battery were replaced by conventional ones. The structure of Coalhouse Fort was strengthened in certain parts and its fire power capability was greatly increased to what it had previously been. Although the Fort was manned during the First World War by both artillery and engineering units, it played almost a supporting role to other defences located further along the river.

With the beginning of the war the 2nd Company of the Royal Garrison Artillery was assigned to look after the Fort's guns, whilst the 2nd Company of the London Light Company was assigned to look after the searchlights.

Mines were placed strategically across the Thames to provide extra protection from any potential invaders. There were also special restrictions placed on friendly vessels which needed to legitimately use the particular stretch of the river.

The River Examinations Service was tasked with enforcing these restrictions with the help of HMS *Champion*, an old wooden warship, which was moored in the middle of the river between Coalhouse Fort on the Essex side and the Cliffe Forts on the Kent side of the river.

The Royal Garrison Artillery, who were stationed at the Fort, were authorised to fire warning shots across the bows of any suspect vessels or those which refused to be stopped and boarded so that their documents could be checked for any irregularities, whilst at the same time allowing those tasked with carrying out the checks, to do so in comparative safety.

In 1962 Thurrock Urban District Council acquired Coalhouse Fort from the Ministry of Defence with the intention of developing it as a riverside amenity. Regrettably this never happened and over the years it fell into disrepair. It became vandalised, overgrown with grass and trees and a hangout for miscreant youngsters. In 1983 the site was taken over by the Coalhouse Fort Project, a group of volunteers who wanted to preserve, restore and maintain the Fort for the benefit of the public so that it wasn't lost in the annals of history. That is exactly what they have managed to do for the past thirty years. The Coalhouse Fort of today is an extremely impressive edifice with a presence and a look of invincibility about it from whichever angle it is approached. Its outer walls which are constructed from large granite blocks, make it a formidable defensive structure.

The Fort sits on higher ground and at a strategic point as the coastline bends sharply round to the left, therefore not only providing it with a more advantageous position over the adjacent River Thames, but making it harder to physically attack with ground troops.

The footpath depicted in the photograph on p.209 takes a route from the Fort directly out to the River Thames; it was built over the top of an existing railway line which allowed for the speedy delivery of supplies.

The above plaque is located on the south side of the nearby St Catherine's Church in memory of those officers, NCOs and men who were stationed at Coalhouse Fort and who gave their lives for their country in the Great War. Remarkably it also commemorates Gordon of Khartoum, who as the Officer Commanding Royal Engineers (OCRE) Gravesend, built Coalhouse Fort in 1869.

Also included on the same memorial is reference to a naval battle with the Dutch off Tilbury in 1667, during which the south aisle of the church along with the vicarage, were both destroyed, one would assume by the Dutch whilst firing their guns at Coalhouse Fort.

Afterword

We hope you have enjoyed this brief tour of Thurrock during the First World War and have found the book to be useful in your own future research.

There are hundreds of names on the memorials which we have included in the book but have not gone into in any detail about. If you wish to do your own research on one of these individuals, then use websites such as www.cwgc.org or www.ancestry.co.uk, both of which you will find extremely helpful.

Where we have included work originally carried out by other parties, we have done so with their permission and rightfully acknowledge their assistance and co-operation in the compilation of this book. If at any stage we have unwittingly omitted to do so then we apologise for the oversight, but we have made every attempt to contact owners of any copyrighted material to seek their permission to use articles or information in the pages of this book.

Index